話說淡水
Let's Talk about Tamsui

中文・英文對照
Chinese-English Interlinear

編著 / 吳錫德　　翻譯 / 吳岳峰　　插畫 / 陳吉斯

淡江大學出版中心

市長序

淡水擁有秀麗的河海景觀、豐富的人文意象，素為臺灣的代表性據點之一，也是許多人心靈的原鄉。回顧歷史，淡水曾經是臺灣的第一大港，也是北臺灣最早接觸到西方文明之處，而幾百年發展的沉澱，也造就淡水今日「世界遺產潛力點」的實力。新北市政府一定盡全力讓這片土地上的珍貴資產，能得到妥善的保存，讓更多人能意識到文明累積之不易，進而去探究巍峨建築背後，所蘊藏著一則又一則的動人故事。

自 1950 年在淡水創校迄今已逾一甲子的淡江大學，是臺灣相當重要的高等學府，孕育無數優秀人才。由淡江大學來出版《話說淡水》多語導覽手冊，可以說是再洽當也不過，這本手冊包含英、西、法、德、日、俄等不同外語的譯本，展現國際化、資訊化及未來化的教育觀，可以幫助國際友人了解淡水，更可以提高淡水的國際能見度。

值《話說淡水》付梓之際，期待本書成為世界各地人士深入認識臺灣的入門磚，也藉由淡水豐富資源之躍然紙上，呈現新北市的地靈人傑，鼓勵人們積極探訪這座無盡藏的美麗城市。

新北市 市長

Preface by the Mayor

Tamsui, a land of magnificent scenery and rich culture, has always been the rare kind of its own and the hometown to numerous courageous souls. Through the ages, Tamsui, the earliest gateway to the Western civilization, used to be the No.1 port of Taiwan. Its centenarian evolution sublimes Tamsui up into Potential World Heritage Site. Highly concerned with the preservation of the cultural and historical assets in Tamsui, the New Taipei City Government will spare no efforts to get the profound value in civilization, history and nature over to the public.

Tamkang University has spanned over six decades in age ever since 1950 when it was first founded. As one of the chief and principal educational institutes of Taiwan, Tamkang University is more than eligible in publishing Let's Talk about Tamsui, a multi-language tourism handbook. The polyglot versions-English, Spanish, French, German, Japanese and Russian-crystallize the educational philosophy in globalization, computerization and futurization and further advance Tamsui's bondage and visibility on the international stage.

In the time when Let's Talk about Tamsui is to be submitted to publication, the work is anticipated to be the global window to Taiwan. And the picturesque, lexical interpretation characterizes the energetic New Taipei City and above all encourages explorations into this Shangri-la city.

Chu, Li-luan, New Taipei City Mayor

目次

Contents

Tamsui 01

歷史上的淡水

淡水，台灣最富傳奇色彩的山城河港。數百年來，接納一波波
來自南海及中國大陸的移民，人來人往，蒼海桑田。

這些豐富有趣、變化萬千的時空故事，直到今天都仍然保留著
彌足珍貴的痕跡。從淡水對岸的觀音山頂上眺望，在長河、山
丘與大海之間，淡水迷人的「山城河港」特色一覽無遺。三百
年前的古城堡、傳統的老街古廟、異國風情的洋樓、豐富多樣
的美景，甚至岸邊急駛而過的捷運班車，還有悠閒漫遊的自行
車群……這一切既幸福，又愜意！

淡水在哪裡？

淡水在台北盆地西北方，濱臨台灣海峽，為淡水河的出海口。東邊與台北市北投相接，北與三芝為鄰，南方則隔淡水河與八里對望。境內多為大屯火山的餘脈散佈，是為五虎崗。只有南邊沿淡水河岸有狹小的平原。

新淡水八景

1. 埔頂攬勝（紅毛城一帶之埔頂地區）
2. 大屯飛翠（大屯山）
3. 沙崙看海（沙崙海灘）
4. 水岸畫影（淡水河岸）
5. 紅樹傍橋（紅樹林、關渡大橋）
6. 河口霞天（淡水河口）
7. 觀音水月（觀音山）
8. 滬街訪古（淡水老街）

「淡水」的由來

據歷史學者陳宗仁考證，古時中國船隻航行各地必須補充淡水，「淡水」意指可停留補充淡水之地。17 世紀，西方殖民勢力進入東亞，台灣位居東亞貿易轉運點，做為北台灣重要河港的淡水其地位更形重要。「淡水」之名亦紛紛出現於當時西方人編製的地圖與文獻典籍中，常見拼法有「Tanchui、Tamchuy」（西班牙語）、「Tamsuy」（荷蘭語）等。這些皆由「淡水」音轉而來，顯見至 17 世紀當時「淡水」一名已被接受成為慣稱，而當時「淡水」的範圍泛指淡水河口附近海面、淡水港及其周邊地域。

「滬尾」之意

滬尾為淡水古名，關於「滬尾」地名由來概有四說:(一)滬魚說、(二)魚尾說、(三)石滬說、(四)原住民音轉說。歷史學者張建隆撰有〈滬尾地名考辨〉一文，指出一份繪於雍正年間的《臺灣附澎湖群島圖》，圖中可見淡水營西方標有「滬尾社」之名，進一步證明滬尾名稱是由原住民音轉而來。

尋奇對話

Q 這裡取名「淡水」還真有趣？

A 這個名字的由來有好幾種說法：一說是漢人船民能在這裡找到淡水，所以才這樣稱呼這裡。另一個古名叫「滬尾」（Hobe），應該就是這裡的最早原住民的名稱。

Q 繼漢人之後，還有哪些國家的勢力來過這裡？

A 最早是荷蘭人，接著有西班牙人、法國人、英國人，最後就是日本人。日本人因為打敗了清廷，獲得割地賠償，佔領台灣 50 年，直到 1945 年才還給漢人。

Q 現在這裡就是漢人的社會，人口幾乎都是漢人！漢人是什麼時間大量移入的？

A 這裡離中國大陸很近，最近的只有 130 公里。從 18 世紀起即已有大批大陸沿海的居民非法並大批遷移至此。淡水就是進入北台灣的唯一大港。清廷最後在 1885 年正式將台灣畫入版圖，設置省會。

Q 美國好萊塢電影公司曾在此拍製一部電影,片名叫做《聖保羅砲艇》(The Sand Pebbles),由史迪夫‧麥昆(Steve McQueen)主演?

A 是的。那是 1965 年在淡水拍攝的。這裡做為 1926 年中國大陸長江的背景。美國這艘船艦捲入中國內戰的故事。

Q 所以淡水應該有許多歷史古蹟?

A 是的。這裡有許多比台灣其他城市還更多、更豐富的古蹟。而且文藝活動也很活躍。現在更是北台灣重要的觀光及休閒城鎮。

渡
船
頭

淡水渡船碼頭是古代漢人移入北台灣的最大港口，早年這裡也是內河航運的轉口。二三百年前風帆點點，魚貫入港，人聲鼎沸的場景只留在畫冊或傳說裡。日據時代基隆港取代它的海運地位，1982 年關渡大橋通車後，渡輪逐漸沒落，僅剩淡水至八里的渡船仍繼續營運。藍色船身的機動交通船悠閒地來回兩地，一副與世無爭、世外桃源的景致。及至 2004 年浮動式碼頭完工，以及藍色公路的開闢，便利觀光小船停靠，銜接漁人碼頭、八里渡船頭、八里左岸或關渡碼頭，帶動全新且現代式的旅遊觀光潮。

淡水渡輪

淡水渡船碼頭是古代北台灣的主要
口岸，自古船來船往，絡繹不絕。
新式客船碼頭於 2004 年 7 月完工，
浮動式碼頭便利觀光小船停靠，帶
動淡水水運交通及觀光效益。

遊船銜接鄰近景點漁人碼頭、八里左
岸，不僅可以延伸遊玩範圍，更可從河上一覽陸地風光。傍晚時分，
夕陽灑落河面，波光粼粼，遠方的觀音山猶如一幅巨型的山水畫。在此
搭上渡輪，觀賞淡水河岸與遠方的關渡大橋，別有一番風貌。除了有山、
海、河、城的多重景觀，每到夕陽西下，河面變成了金黃色。夜晚，明
月映照河面，白色水光令人心搖神馳。

藍色公路

「藍色公路」的發想是開發淡水河及
基隆河的觀光河運，自 2004 年 2
月開航，目前已有 8 條內河航線，
載客量已超過 100 萬人次。沿途有
導覽說明，尤其可近距離觀看河面
生態，十分知性及愜意。另外，由
淡水出發，亦規劃有北台灣藍色公路及北海岸藍色
公路兩條海上藍色公路航線，是延伸淡水觀光範圍及提供更多元休閒旅
遊的設計。

為吸引日籍觀光客搭乘，更開發出全日語導覽行程。對岸台北港更規劃
有直航大陸福州的船班，以引進更多的陸客。

淡水夕陽

淡水山河交接，西向背東，每逢日落時分，浩浩江水映著滿天霞光，氣象萬千。自古不知引發多少騷人墨客歌詠，亦不知吸引多少畫家攝影屏息讚嘆。尤其每逢秋高氣爽時節，霞光鋪天蓋地而來，映著整座河岸城鎮，灑落在每個行人遊客身上，令人滿心幸福，流連忘返。

〈流浪到淡水〉

作詞、作曲 / 陳明章　編曲 / China Blue

有緣　無緣　大家來作伙
燒酒喝一杯　乎乾啦　乎乾啦
扞著風琴　提著吉他　雙人牽作伙　為著生活流浪到淡水
想起故鄉心愛的人　感情用這厚　才知影癡情是第一憨的人
燒酒落喉　心情輕鬆　鬱卒放棄捨　往事將伊當作一場夢
想起故鄉　心愛的人　將伊放抹記　流浪到他鄉　重新過日子
阮不是喜愛虛華　阮只是環境來拖磨
人客若叫阮　風雨嘛著行　為伊唱出留戀的情歌
人生浮沈　起起落落　毋免來煩惱　有時月圓　有時也抹平
趁著今晚歡歡喜喜　鬥陣來作伙　你來跳舞　我來唸歌詩
有緣　無緣　大家來作伙
燒酒喝一杯　乎乾啦　乎乾啦　（重覆三次）

15

尋奇對話

Q 到淡水真的很方便！從台北車站到這裡只花了 35 分鐘，而且沿途風景很不錯！

A 現在台北的捷運網越來越密集，越方便，可以吸引更遠方的旅客。所以每逢週末或假日，這裡可說「遊人如織」。

Q 除了捷運連接，其他交通路線好像也很方便。

A 從台北市區到這裡也可以走公路或水路。不過，對不開車的人來講，搭乘捷運是最方便的。捷運是 1997 年通車的，原先的路基是日本人興建的淡水火車支線，從 1901 年行駛到 1988 年。

Q 我們也可以搭船到淡水！

A 是的！2005 年起，旅客可以從台北舊市區大稻埕上船，一路遊覽到淡水，甚至到出海口的「漁人碼頭」。2007 年起，還可以搭乘一艘仿古的美式餐船「大河號」，一路吃喝休閒觀光到淡水！

Q 淡水好像人口也很多，而且年輕人特別多！

A 淡水區的人口有 15 萬餘人，實際應更多。因為有 5 所大學之故，流動人口相當多。加上緊臨台北，交通便捷，房價也比較低些，很多年輕夫婦就選在淡水定居。

Q 來此地觀光的旅客應該也很多吧？

A 「淡水夕照」一直是台灣八景之一，自古觀光旅客就很多。目前它還是名列觀光客最喜歡一遊的十大觀光景點。淡水地區每年吸引觀光客達 500 萬人次。

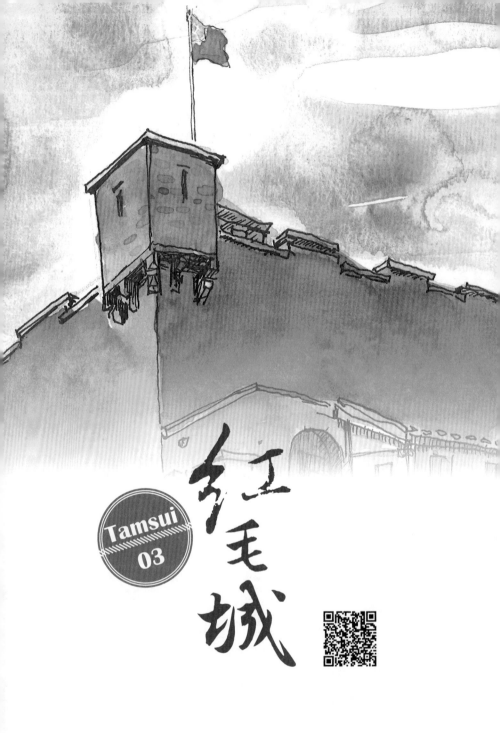

Tamsui 03

紅毛城

紅毛城，1628 年由當時佔領台灣北部的西班牙人所建。1644 年荷蘭人於原址予以重建。因漢人稱荷蘭人為「紅毛」，當地人習稱此地為「紅毛城」。鄭成功擊退荷蘭人，短暫經營此地，清廷亦加以整修，做為防禦要塞。1867 年被英國長期租用，當作領事館辦公地點，並於 1891 年在其後方建成一座維多利亞風格之建物，做為領事公邸。1972 年英國與我國斷交撤館，轉交澳大利亞及美國托管，一直到 1980 年，該城產權才轉到我國。紅毛城為台灣現存最古老的建築之一，也是國定一級古蹟。2005 年 7 月整建後改為「淡水古蹟博物館」。

〈滬尾紅毛城〉

〔…〕遠望濤頭一線而至，聲隆隆如雷，令人作吞雲夢八九之想。頃之，夕陽向西下，金光閃爍，氣象萬千，所有兩崖煙雲竹樹、風帆沙鳥，一齊收入樓台中，層見迭出，不使人一覽可盡，洋洋奇觀哉……。

吳子光，苗栗銅鑼人，清同治年間舉人，經通經史子集，被譽為「1900年前台灣第一學問家」。丘逢甲即其弟子。1866年，他於淡水候船赴大陸應試，閒遊此地，撰文〈滬尾紅毛城〉。

荷蘭城堡

即「紅毛城」主樓，原址為西班牙所建，原以木頭築成，因曾被漢人焚毀，於1637年改以石材重建。工事完成不久，西班牙決定撤軍，下令摧毀該城。荷蘭駐軍於1644年5月動工重建。除了石材，還遠道自印尼運來上好石灰與磚頭，挖深地基，也使用穹窿式構造，證明荷蘭人有心要建造一座堅固的城堡。1662年鄭成功驅逐了南部荷蘭人，淡水之守軍亦隨之撤走。1863由英國人租用，將此炮城改為領事辦公室、住宅及四間牢房。

英國領事館公邸

淡水英國領事公邸為紅磚造陽台殖民地樣式建築,有獨特熱帶地區防暑的拱廊設計,斜屋頂等特徵,由當時駐淡水英國領事聘請英國建築師設計,紅磚及匠師可能來自福建廈門。領事公邸底樓西側為客廳及書房,東側為餐廳及廚房,後側為洗衣間及數間傭人房。二樓有三間大臥室及貯藏室。四周綠地,闢有玫瑰園,公邸迴廊是喝下午茶的場所。淡水領事公邸用材極為講究,設計雅致,是大英帝國在東亞地區僅存少數的較早期洋樓。

尋奇對話

Q 英國人也應該是漢人眼中的「紅毛」吧？

A 是的。過去我們中國人一向稱外國人為「紅毛仔」，因為西方的白人都有一頭紅棕色頭髮。紅毛城將近 400 年的歷史中，先後被西班牙、荷蘭、明鄭成功、清朝、英國、日本、美國、澳洲的經營。認識紅毛城，等於走一趟台灣近代史。

Q 英國人在台灣一共蓋了幾間「領事館」？

A 一共三間。最早一間在高雄，其次是安平，淡水這間應是最晚蓋成的，規模應該是最大的，視野及維護應該也是最好的。不過，三間的風格都很類似，即維多利亞式，俗稱「殖民地式建築」。

Q 當時領事館業務應該很龐大吧？

A 1860 年開放淡水為國際通商港埠後，台灣的對外貿易就遽增了很多。尤其是茶業和樟腦的出口。主要是輸往中國大陸。

Q 1895 年日本殖民台灣，英國人還留下來嗎？

A 是的。依國際法這塊地還是屬於英國政府。所以英國人繼續留下來。直到第二次世界大戰期間才撤走。戰後他們又回來向中華民國政府索回。

Q 英國人為何遲至 1980 年才肯交回這塊地？

A 英國人應該一直都捨不得交出這塊地。即便 1972 年他們就與我國斷交，還是在法理上繼續擁有這塊地。我們是費了很多努力才要回它的。不然，我們今天也不可能上這兒來的！

Tamsui
04

馬偕、教會、學校

加拿大人馬偕是淡水最知名的外國人，有一條街以他的名字命名，由他一手創辦的馬偕紀念醫院至今還日夜在服務成千上萬的台灣人。他一輩子行醫、傳教、興學，幾乎以淡水為家，前後近 30 年。最後歿於斯，葬於斯。馬偕 27 歲時離開家鄉，1872 年 3 月抵達淡水，就決定在此落腳，宣教基督長老教會。他自美加兩地募款，興建醫館，中法滬尾之役，協助照料清廷傷兵；他沒有牙科醫學訓練，卻幫台灣人拔了 2 萬多顆蛀牙。他還自國外輸入蔬菜種子：蘿蔔、甘藍菜、蕃茄、花椰菜、胡蘿蔔等。

淡水禮拜堂

淡水禮拜堂，位於馬偕街上。目前的建物改建於
1932 年，由馬偕之子偕叡廉（George W. Mac-
kay） 所設計，為仿歌德式的紅磚建築，有一方
型鐘塔，內部為木架天花板，且保存一個自 1909
年開始使用的古風琴。淡水禮拜堂是淡水地區最
大的台灣基督教長老教會聚會所，約可容納 300
人。此教堂曾在 1986 年修建屋頂。教堂外觀以
極佳品質的紅磚構成，且牆面變化有序，據傳出
自於當年設計名匠洪泉、黃阿樹之手。這座教堂
幾乎是早年淡水的地標，同時也是畫家最愛入畫
的寫生美景。

馬偕傳教士

馬偕（George Leslie Mackay，1844-1901），
生於加拿大安大略省，醫師與長老教會牧師。
台灣人稱其「馬偕博士」或「偕牧師」。西方
歷史學者以「寧願燒盡，不願朽壞」（Rather
burn than rust out）讚賞馬偕的一生。1871
年底到達高雄，隔年起在淡水開始傳教，學習
閩南話，之後還娶了台灣女子為妻。他四處旅
行傳播基督福音，在台灣北部及東部設立二十
餘個教會。1882 年創建牛津學堂（今真理大
學）。2 年後又建立第一個供女子就讀的婦學
堂。其子偕叡廉承接衣缽，創辦了淡江中學。
著有《馬偕日記》，70 多萬字，分 3 冊出版。

淡江中學

淡江中學正式於 1914 年創設，昔稱淡水中學、淡水高女，為加拿大長老教會宣教士馬偕博士父子所創，是台灣罕見的百年老校。不僅其校史見證台灣歷史遞嬗與教育文化變遷。其校園座落依山面海，風光秀麗，綠意盎然。該校建築以歐美名校為藍本，並融入中國傳統建築元素，提供了啟發及培養人文思想的最佳環境。「八角塔」融合了中國的寶塔和西方拜占庭式建築，是淡江中學精神堡壘，由該校幾何老師加拿大宣教士羅虔益（K. W. Dowie）所設計，1925 年 6 月峻工。

尋奇對話

Q 我注意到淡水老市區有一條「馬偕街」，路口的圓環還樹立著馬偕先生的半身雕像。這位加拿大人應該就是淡水的榮譽市民囉！

A 是啊！馬偕博士在台灣30年，以淡水為根據地，一輩子行醫、傳教、興學不遺餘力，造福台灣人甚多！

Q 相對於西班牙、荷蘭，以及後來的法國及日本的強佔，英國人的唯利是圖，這位加拿大人的做法的確教人欽佩！

A 馬偕博士將現代醫學引進到台灣，幫台灣人治病療傷，培養台灣人醫學技術。籌資開設醫院，目前已發展到一所大型現代醫院「馬偕紀念醫院」，全省共有四個分院、3000多個床位、近7000員工。同時還設立馬偕護校及馬偕醫學院。

Q 聽說淡江中學很美，也是著名歌手及作曲家周杰倫的母校？

A 淡江中學可說是台灣最早的一所西式學堂，校舍建築美輪美奐，校園景緻優美，與淡水華人社區相映成趣。他也是馬偕博士所興辦，由其子克紹箕裘。這所中學相當開放，培養許多藝文及經貿人才，包括前總統李登輝也是這裡畢業的！

Q 聽說淡江大學的興辦與它也有關連？

A 是的。淡江大學創辦人張驚聲從日本留學，自大陸返鄉，很想興辦一所大學。他先應聘擔任淡江中學校長，後來順利集資購地，才在 1950 年創立淡江大學。它最初的校址還設在淡江中學裡！

Q 周杰倫好像在這裡拍了一部電影？

A 那部電影叫做《不能說的秘密》（2007）。事實上，淡水一直是電影青睞的拍攝場景，像早期的《聖保羅炮艇》（1966），以及較近的《我們的天空》（1986）、《問男孩》（2008），還有一齣電視劇《青梅竹馬》（2009）等等。

Tamsui
05

觀音山

觀音山位於淡水河出海口左岸，海拔標高616公尺，山頂稱「硬漢嶺」，區內有多座古剎，更增添此山的靈性，其中還有數間供奉觀世音菩薩的觀音寺。西臨台灣海峽，東北隔淡水河遠望關渡，昔日的「坌嶺吐霧」為淡水八大景之一，是登山及健行的好去處。荷蘭統治時代，叫淡水山（Tamswijse berch），但漢人習稱八里坌山，因山邊的原住民部落八里坌社而得名。改稱「觀音山」的說法有二：一說是1752年貢生胡焯猷在山路籌建大士觀而得名，一說是由於山稜起伏變化，從關渡一帶眺望時，山形起伏貌似觀音菩薩的面容仰天的側面而得名。

觀音傳奇

觀世音菩薩（梵文：**अवलोकितेश्वर**，Avalokiteśvara），又譯為觀自在菩薩，簡稱「觀音菩薩」，這位佛教神祇是東亞民間普遍敬仰崇拜的菩薩，也是中國民間信仰所崇信的「家堂五神」的首尊，台灣民眾常將之繪製於家堂神畫「佛祖漆」上，與自家所祀神明一同晨昏祭祀。佛教的經典上說觀世音菩薩的悲心廣大，世間眾生無論遭遇何種災難，若一心稱念觀世音菩薩聖號，菩薩即時尋聲赴感，使之離苦得樂，故人稱「大慈大悲觀世音菩薩」，為佛教中知名度最高的大菩薩，有「家家阿彌陀，戶戶觀世音」的讚譽。

福佑宮

福佑宮是淡水最老的廟宇，1732 年左右應已草創，1796 年重建迄今。廟內供奉媽祖，是早期乘船移民及商貿的守護神祇。也是早期全淡水的信仰中心。廟口兩側街道是淡水最早的街衢。大前方即為舊時登岸碼頭。這裡也是淡水發展的起點。中法戰爭期間（1884~85）該廟因佑護漢人免招法國海軍的進侵，獲光緒皇帝頒贈「翌天昭佑」匾額。福佑宮被列為三級古蹟，廟中有古匾額、石柱、石碑等歷史文物。其中 1796 年刻製的「望高樓碑誌」即記載淡水商賈籌建燈塔事蹟。

十三行博物館

十三行博物館位於今淡水河左岸出海口，為一座考古博物館，二級古蹟。1957 年地質學者林朝棨勘查後定名為「十三行遺址」，後經考古學者陸續發掘出極具代表性之文物及墓葬等，為距今 1800 年至 500 年前臺灣史前鐵器時代之代表文化。其人種可能與平埔族中凱達格蘭族有關。出土重要文物為陶器、鐵器、煉鐵爐、墓葬品及與外族之交易品等。1989 年動工興建，2003 年 4 月開館營運。博物館週邊區域具豐富多樣的遺址古蹟、自然保留區、水岸景觀、歷史民俗、產業文化及公共設施等資源，串聯成為「淡水河八里左岸文化生態園區」。

尋奇對話

Q 這裡為什麼叫做「十三行」？

A 因為清末有十三家洋行在這裡設了分行，當地人就稱它「十三行」。

Q 早期這裡的居民應該都是大航海家囉？

A 是的。台灣的所有原住民都是大航海家的後裔！16 族原住民是在不同時期，算準洋流從大陸沿海或鄰近島嶼，坐上「獨木船」（Banka），冒著身命危險，飄洋過海而來的。此地的原住民生活在 1500~2000 年前，是北台灣平埔族當中凱達格蘭族祖先。

Q 現在這裡可以直航到中國大陸嗎？

A 是的。從 2013 年 10 月起，從台北港（八里）便可直航到福州（平潭）。只要花上 3 個小時。過去漢人坐帆船過來，可要花上好幾天！

Q 觀世音菩薩是男？還是女？

A 按照佛教的說法，佛是中性的，大菩薩也是中性的。其實，唐朝的觀世音菩薩是男相。可能祂經常化身女性指點眾生之故，更可能祂救苦救難是母愛的象徵之故。

Q 「媽祖」是誰啊？

A 相傳她是宋朝福建漁家的女子林默娘，因捨身救起船難的父兄，而有了海上拯救者的形象。媽祖信仰遍及華南沿海各地及東南亞，信眾超過2億人。單單台灣就有超過900座伺奉的廟宇。

淡水河岸

Tamsui
06

從老街至小漁港間長 1.5 公里的淡水河沿岸，區公所命名為「金
色水岸」。因為晚霞時分，這裡經常會被夕陽照得金碧輝煌。
一路有林蔭步道、親水河岸、水上舞台、咖啡座椅區、觀潮灣、
觀潮藝術廣場等設施，小漁港的 8 棵百年榕樹是民眾最喜歡的
乘涼、垂釣、觀賞夕陽的地方。商家捐贈余蓮春的〈戲魚〉，
上原一明的〈舟月〉，賴哲祥的〈迎曦〉等三件藝術雕塑品更
增添了河堤的藝術氣息。河岸沿路商家林立，特色咖啡館、異
國餐廳、創意商店毗連而立，是休閒散心的最佳去處。

民歌響起

「民歌」來自民間由國人自行填詞、作曲、演唱的流行歌曲。最初在大學校園裡傳唱，故也叫「校園民歌」。它是一股社會的反省力量，尤其來自彼時年輕人內心的吶喊。從 1970 年代末起風行全台，是台灣本土意識的併發及文藝創作能量的引爆。當中帶頭的靈魂人物就是淡江大學校友的李雙澤（1949~1977）。1976 年，他在淡大校園的一場演唱會上，帶著一瓶可口可樂走上台，問台下的觀眾：「無論歐美還是台灣，喝的都是可口可樂，聽的都是洋文歌，請問我們自己的歌在那裡？」在一片詫異中，他拿起吉他唱起李臨秋先生（1909~1979）填詞的歌謠〈補破網〉，當下引起熱情的共鳴。

水岸畫影

淡水小鎮，山河海交接，風景壯麗。昔為北方大港，人文歷史韻味深厚。復以開埠甚早，往來交通，東西文化交織，多元特色，極易引發詩人墨客歌詠，畫家攝景。日據時代起，尤其吸引專業畫家至此作畫寫生，素有台灣畫家「朝聖地」之美名。它自成一格的「歐洲小鎮翦影」，美洲風格的哥特教堂、停泊岸邊的船隻、水中行駛的渡輪、山巒起伏的觀音群山、或霧靄茫茫的河口風景都能一一入畫。台灣最早一代的西畫家幾乎無人不曾蒞此，並留下歷久彌新的淡水風光。

葉俊麟的發想……

1957年，擔任編劇的葉俊麟先生隨外景隊來到淡水，黃昏時他沿著河邊獨行。落日慢慢沉入海面，居民擠在渡船口迎接歸來的漁船。忽有歌聲隱約斷續傳來，他尋覓歌聲來處，抬頭望見不遠斜坡上的閣樓，一名女子佇候在門後，遙望渡船口一家和樂的場景，那女子的神情觸動了他寫下這首傳唱不墜的名曲。……

〈淡水暮色〉

作詞/葉俊麟　作曲/洪一峰，1957

日頭將要沉落西　水面染五彩
男女老幼在等待　漁船倒返來
桃色樓窗門半開　琴聲訴悲哀 啊……
幽怨的心情無人知。
朦朧月色白光線　浮出紗帽山
河流水影色變換　海風陣陣寒
一隻小鳥找無伴　歌在船頭岸 啊……
美妙的啼叫動心肝。
淡水黃昏帶詩意　夜霧罩四邊
教堂鐘聲心空虛　響對海面去
埔頂燈光真稀微　閃閃像天星 啊……
難忘的情景引人悲。

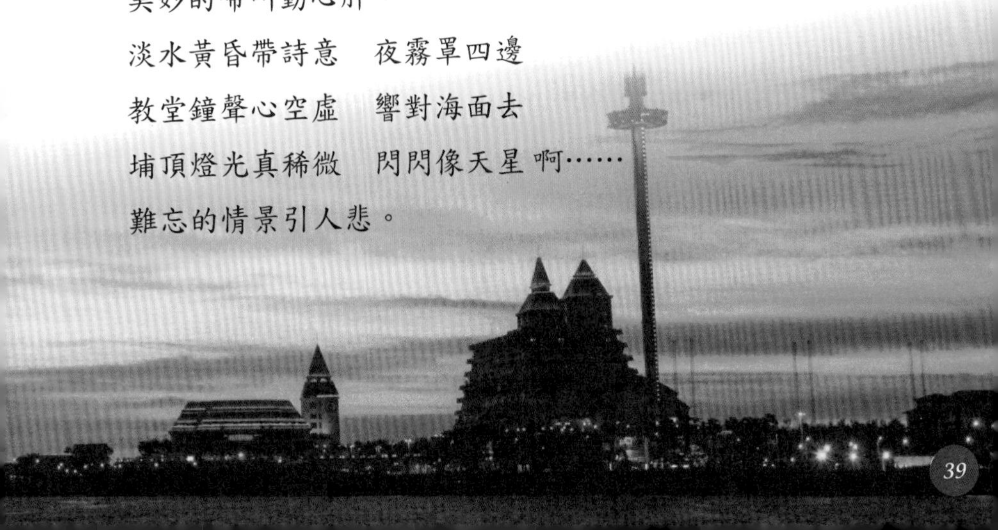

尋奇對話

Q 這裡這麼多遊客，應該都是捷運載來的吧？

A 是的。捷運淡水線 1997 年通車，初期很少人搭乘，還賠了錢。如今班班客滿，星期假日更是「一位難求」。

Q 淡水最多可容納多少觀光客？

A 2014 年春節期間，因為天氣晴朗、溫暖，創下單日超過 10 萬人紀錄！整個河堤及老街擠得寸步難行，從高處看，簡直像一堆沙丁魚群。

Q 這樣那能做休閒及觀光？

A 大概只能湊熱鬧、看人潮吧！其實，非假日或清早，淡水是很寧靜且悠閒的。

Q 民歌由淡水出發，很多人也寫歌來歌頌淡水。淡水有沒有音樂學院？

A 只有遠在關渡的國立台北藝術大學設有音樂學系，其他學校都沒有。但這不礙事啊！淡水讓人真情流露，很容易就讓會人創作出貼近庶民的歌曲。譬如 1997 年陳明章先生作曲填詞的〈流浪到淡水〉就紅遍全台大街小巷。

Q 淡水河邊跟以前有何不一樣？

A 就我印象所及，以前這裡只是個小漁港，魚腥味很重，遊客不多。現在河岸（包括對岸八里的河堤）整治了很多，變成了觀光休閒河岸，很現代感，也很商業化！

淡水老街

Tamsui
07

淡水曾是北台灣第一大港，因基隆港開通及泥沙淤積，逐漸喪失商務功能，迅速沒落成為一座地方小漁港，現已轉型為觀光休閒小鎮。中正路老街一帶，雖新式樓房林立，依然可見到許多老式磚造店舖，反映出本地的開發史。古老寺廟林立，漫步在坡道間，造訪淡水老街應能體驗先民的生活點滴。老街位於中正路、重建街、清水街等一帶，因鄰近淡水捷運站，交通方便，每到假日總是人山人海。尤其中正路，堪稱淡水最熱鬧的街道。老街區也集美食、小吃、老街為一身，近年來更因不少古董店及民藝品店進駐，也營造出民俗色彩與懷舊風味。

重建街

矗立山崙上的重建街是淡水歷史
悠久的老街，也是發展最早的商
業街，更是外地人體驗淡水山
城味道最好的一條街道。重建
街原本是一條蜿蜒五、六百
公尺的歷史街道，是昔日的
「頂街」，當年是陸路交通的要道，
往下直通碼頭，往上連接山丘上方的聚落村莊。從
19世紀末的50年一直是繁榮鼎盛。不少淡水著名政治、金融、教
育界的名人都是世居此地。由於建在起伏不平的山坡上，房屋與路面常
形成高低落差，相當特別。如今還保存幾間舊式長條形街屋，古意盎然。

讚滿重建街！

〔中國時報 / 2013.12.02 / 謝幸恩 報
導〕超過230年歷史的淡水重建街，
仍保有四處以上古蹟，但新北市政府
因公共安全疑慮，年底推動第二階段
拓寬工程，文史工作者在網路上發起
「讚滿重建街」活動，1日吸引數百
位支持者以柔性訴求，希望市府讓
重建街「原地保留」。短短380公
尺餘，全以石階堆砌而成，一路蜿蜒而上，可
見兩側饒富人文氣息的古厝。地方居民說，有的房子可見到中法戰爭時
所留下的彈孔，見證了淡水的興衰。

白樓

淡水「白樓」原本坐落淡水三民街週邊坡地，約建於 1875 年，外牆白灰因而得名。據傳為板橋富商林本源出資，由馬偕博士門生嚴清華所建，再租予猶太商行，之後曾改作一般公寓雜院。白樓在 1992 年因失火，而拆除改建。由於它曾是許多老輩畫家的入畫題材，如今只能在這些畫作裡尋得它的風采。2009 年，淡水文化基金會特別委託彩墨畫家蕭進興在最接近白樓舊址上坡路段，利用右側牆壁，畫下白樓舊觀，並延伸至周遭景致。這堵長卷式壁畫，耗費數月始完工，可一覽無遺俯瞰淡水，堪稱淡水最生動、最震憾人心的公共藝術。

紅樓

該建築原是船商李貽和的宅第，與已經拆除的「白樓」齊名。1899 年落成，由於李貽和所經營的兩艘貨船發生撞沉意外，在 1913 年轉賣給時任台北廳參事的洪以南。洪以南在成為這棟紅樓的主人後，為它取了「達觀樓」的雅號。

紅樓採西方洋樓式風格，與淡水英國領事館公邸外觀相近，其屋前寬闊庭院，四周輔以小徑、階梯相通，為早年景觀最佳之房舍。直至 1963 年，轉賣給德裕魚丸的洪炳堅夫婦。1999 年年初整修紅樓，期間曾多方請教建築、歷史、藝術等專家學者。於 2000 年元月正式對外營業，成了一家複合式餐廳與藝文館。

尋奇對話

Q 這些藝文人士呼籲保存老街的溫和訴求很有意思。他們是怎麼湊在一起的？

A 在台灣每個有歷史的城鎮都會自發地組成「文史工作室」，定期有些討論及表達。我想他們是透過網路集結的。

Q 聽說台灣的臉書人口密度是世界最高之一？

A 現在使用 Line 的人也越來越多了。以前搭車，車箱內很喧嘩。現在即便人很多也很安靜，因為男女老少都在滑手機！

Q 重建街的上坡階梯很有古意，也很特殊。因為每一階梯都不會太高，走起來也不致於太累。

A 是啊！這些階梯都有一、二百年的歷史，也不知道有多少人從上面走過。我們可以想像當年人聲鼎沸的場景……。因為要上下貨的關係，所以每個台階都不會做得太高，連老人家來走都沒問題。

Q 「讚滿重建街」這個標語是很棒的雙關語！

A 「讚」與「站」在台灣式國語裡是同音字。「讚」表示「支持、同意」；「站」表示「出席、佔據」。

Q 「紅樓」整修得很細膩，很棒。可以想像當年的氣派及華麗。

A 這裡的景觀特別好，最適宜觀看夕陽及夜景。我請你上去喝杯咖啡吧！

Tamsui
08

殼牌倉庫

殼牌公司（Shell）儲油倉庫和油槽以及英商嘉士洋行倉庫，位於捷運淡水站旁的鼻仔頭，佔地面積約 3000 坪。1894 年 11 月由茶葉外銷洋行「嘉士洋行」所承租，用以經營茶葉貿易。1897 年由殼牌公司買下，並增建四座大型磚造儲油倉庫，並舖設可接通淡水線鐵路的鐵道，大規模經營起煤油買賣。也由於煤油臭氣瀰漫，淡水人稱之為「臭油棧」。直到 1944 年 10 月遭美軍轟炸導致油槽起火，三天三夜才被撲滅。2000 年指定為古蹟，殼牌公司也將此捐贈給淡水文化基金會。2001 年於此創辦「淡水社區大學」。2011 年規劃為「淡水文化園區」。

淡水社區大學

淡水社區大學於 2001 年 8 月正式開學，課程豐富又多樣，有很多大學院校裡不可能出現的課程，收費又特別低廉，是推動公共教育最佳的空間。在它的校務規程中明訂「以促進終身學習，提昇社區文化，參與社區營造，發展公民社會為宗旨」，自我期許要不斷落實教育改革的理念。淡水社區大學的特色就是結合古蹟，再融入在地文化，認識淡水等相關課程。這個學校很自豪，因為他們的教學空間是百年古蹟！

淡水文化園區

淡水文化園區,即殼牌倉庫舊址與週遭綠
地及濕地,經新北市政府修繕完工後,於
2011 年正式對外開放。「淡水文化園區」
占地約 1.8 公頃,園區內有八棟老建物,還
有搬運油品的鐵軌遺跡。修復的八棟建築
物,皆以紅壁磚、土漿疊砌,其中六間是儲
放油品的倉庫,一間幫浦間,另有一間鍋爐
間。經歷過數度經營轉移以及戰火摧殘的市
定古蹟淡水殼牌倉庫,終於以全新的姿態風

華再現。內設有教學中心(淡水社區大學)、展演區、露天舞台、藝文
沙龍、生態區、濕地等空間。

鄞山寺 / 客家會館

鄞山寺,建於 1822 年,二級古蹟,寺內奉
祀定光古佛,定光古佛是中國南方客家人的
祭祀圈才有的信仰。該寺大體上完整保存道
光初年原貌,包括當年施工的的屋脊泥塑都
相當完整。

為現今台灣唯一保存完整的清時會館。會
館就是同鄉會會所,以互相濟助為目的。
主要因為在清道光年間從汀州移居台灣
北部的客家人越來越多,汀州人怕漳
州、泉州人欺負,所以在上岸處集合
形成聚落,並出資蓋地方會館,後續
自唐山渡海來台的人,可臨時落腳寄
居在這樣的地方會館裡。

尋奇對話

Q 把歷史古蹟跟生態環境結合在一起是挺不錯的點子。

A 是的。最重要的還是「管理」。所以政府 2007 年通過設置「鼻仔頭史蹟生態區」,將 5 個歷史古蹟:鄞山寺、湖南勇古墓、淡水殼牌倉庫、淡水水上機場、淡水氣候觀測所,以及周邊的自然生態資源一起納入管理。

Q 台灣人很重視環保和休閒?

A 這是最近 10 幾年的事。尤其是環保署的設置,發揮不少功能。文化部的運作也相當正面。休閒與生態似乎是民眾自覺自發的需求。

Q 感覺上,淡水蠻能與世界接軌的。

A 歷史上的淡水一直都很國際化!現在的台灣不僅民主,也非常開放。不過很多歷史感消失得特別快,歷史的痕跡要特別細心的加以保存!

Q 聽說社區大學裡老人學生特別多？

A 是的。一方面是許多公職人員可以提前退休，他們衣食無慮，身體也夠好，總會想出來參與社會活動。另一方面台灣人的人均壽命提高了，所以老人的需求也增多了。華人社會有句銘言：活到老，學到老！

Q 現在我明白了，淡水除了是年輕人的天堂，將來也可能老年人最愛居住的城市！

A 老實說，淡水還是吵了一點，交通尤其擁擠！除非我們犧牲一點環境，建好交通，才有此可能。

Tamsui
09

滬尾砲台

滬尾砲台位淡水北方，建於 1886 年。佔地約 8 公頃，為台灣首任巡撫劉銘傳所建，以捍衛淡水港。該砲台雖停用多年，因長期屬軍事要塞，保留狀態頗佳。營門上仍留存劉銘傳親筆所題之「北門鎖鑰」碑文。西班牙人也曾在此建造砲台，荷蘭人延用。荷蘭撤走駐軍時曾將之燒毀。清廷在 1808 年加派兵力，駐防該地，1813 年並在現址興築砲台。中法戰爭後，清廷命當時的台灣巡撫劉銘傳加強台海防務。日治時期，日軍撤下當時在滬尾的四門砲塔，將此地改作砲兵練習場地。國民政府重新賦予滬尾砲台國防任務，派兵駐守。1985 核定為二級古蹟，整修後開放民眾遊覽。

油車口

1884年滬尾之役的古戰場，相傳300年前由泉州移民所開闢，18世紀中葉，有郭姓泉州人在此開設油坊因而得名。油車口碼頭則是淡水拍攝婚紗照的熱門景點。此處可一覽觀音山、淡水河、漁船及夕陽，交互搭配，格外秀麗。油車口的忠義宮蘇府王爺廟，是淡水地區最大王爺廟，每年農曆的9月初九重陽節，都會舉辦燒王船的祭典。30多年前廟旁的黑色老厝，曾開一家物美價廉的小吃店，人稱「黑店」，以排骨飯打出名號，後因道路拓寬遷往附近，每逢用餐時刻依然門庭若市，車水馬龍，蔚為奇景。

中法戰爭 / 滬尾戰役

1884 年 8 月，法軍圖佔領北台灣，派軍艦進犯，爆發中法戰爭－滬尾之役。當時台灣巡撫劉銘傳發現淡水重要性，擔心法軍可由淡水河直接進入台北府城，因此決定棄守基隆，把兵力改移至淡水。當時清朝在淡水的沙崙、中崙、油車口修築砲台均遭法艦砲轟摧毀。劉銘傳任命提督孫開華，負責整修淡水防禦工事，以填石塞港，佈置水雷，建造城岸，修築砲台禦敵。10 月 8 日，孫開華帶領清兵及鄉勇，奮勇抗敵，擊退法軍。此為清廷難能可貴之勝戰。法軍後來封鎖海岸半年餘始撤走。

北門鎖鑰

指北城門上的鎖及鑰匙，後借指北方的軍事要地。1885 年滬尾戰後，清廷加強防禦工事。劉銘傳聘請德籍技師巴恩士（Max E. Hecht, 1853-1892）監造，並自英國購入 31 尊大砲，1889 年安裝竣工。惟新砲未曾參與戰事，故基地建築保持相當完整。現存東南方的營門上的碑文「北門鎖鑰」為劉銘傳親筆所提。這也是劉銘傳在台灣本島所建砲台，唯一碩果僅存的一座，具有其特殊的意義與價值。巴恩士也因建成此一海防利器有功，還獲清廷贈勳及賞銀表揚。39 歲歿於台灣，葬於淡水外僑墓園。

尋奇對話

Q 這裡居高臨下，視野極佳，的確是鎮守的好地方。

A 這裡是所謂淡水的「五虎崗」的第一崗，習稱「鳥啾崗」。另一頭就是老淡水高爾夫球場，它是台灣最早一座高爾夫球場，1919 年由日本人建成。原先這塊地還是清軍的練兵場。

Q 湖南人與淡水人還蠻有關連的？

A 當初清廷由大陸調來台灣防守的正規軍一大部份來自湖南。1884 年滬尾之役的守將孫開華也是湖南人。在竿蓁坟場還有一座湖南勇古墓。

Q 台灣很流行婚紗照，聽說還外銷到中國大陸去？

A 婚紗是筆好生意！台北市區還有一條「婚紗街」。大陸的婚紗照幾乎都是台灣業者去開發的。

Q 婚紗照是否一定會選上風景最美的地方拍攝呢？

A 這是所謂的「出外景」，就是戶外婚紗照。當然要選居家附近風景最美的地方拍攝。預算多的還可以安排出國拍攝，順便渡蜜月！所以婚紗攝影師往往就是旅遊景點的最佳探子。

Q 拍了婚紗照是否比較不會離婚呢？

A 過去台灣的離婚率很低，現在比較高些。的確，年輕夫婦如果鬧彆扭，若去翻翻婚紗照，或許就會打消分手的念頭。

Tamsui
10

漁人碼頭

淡水漁人碼頭，位在淡水河出海口東岸，前身為1987年開闢的
淡水第二漁港，鄰近沙崙海水浴場，是淡水最新開發的觀光景
點，於2001年3月正式完工並對外開放，以其夕陽景色及新
鮮的漁貨聞名。目前除了觀光休閒設施之外，仍然保有其漁業
港口的功能。浮動漁船碼頭約可停泊150艘漁船及遊艇，河岸
觀景劇場平台最大能容納3000名觀眾。白色的斜張跨港大橋於
2003年2月14日情人節當天正式啟用，故又稱「情人橋」。
在橋上可欣賞夕陽景色，總長約164.9公尺。水路及陸路交通皆
可通達，有一座5星級景觀旅館。

情人橋

「情人橋」位於漁人碼頭上專供行人步行的跨港景觀大橋。長 164.9 公尺、寬 5 公尺，最高處 12 公尺，微彎的大橋柱側看像似流線船帆造型，遠觀整座橋的色彩是白色，但細看其實是淺白又帶點粉紫與粉紅色的柔美色調。由於大橋的造型優美而浪漫，視野非常遼闊，因此目前已成淡水風景的地標景點。情人橋有個美麗的傳說：情人們若是牽著手、心繫著彼此，相偕走過情人橋，那麼兩人的戀情將更加美麗，但若在走過情人橋的中途，有人回頭了，或把手放開了，那麼未來，他們的戀情將會受到許多考驗。

情人塔

耗資近 3 億多元打造的漁人碼頭「情人塔」於 2011 年 5 月正式啟用，塔高計 100 公尺，每次可容納 80 人，可提供淡水區域 360 度全視野景觀。瑞士製造，耗時 4 年打造，是台灣第一座百米觀景塔，有 360 度的旋轉觀景塔，外加一座可觀賞淡水景色的圓形座艙，座艙外罩為整片式安全玻璃防護罩，可有效防風雨。乘客進入座艙中，座艙會緩緩調整上升與下降的角度，隨著情人塔緩緩旋轉上升，登高望遠，可將淡水美景盡收眼底。

休閒漁港

漁人碼頭雖然能保有漁業港口的功能，但幾乎已轉型為「遊艇碼頭」，它的浮動碼頭上經常停滿各式各樣的小遊艇。它們的主人大多是台北都會裡的富豪人士，因熱愛海上活動，買了遊艇，將這裡當「停船場」，有空才會開出海兜風。這裡是「藍色公路」的重要景點，來自各處的客船都會在此停泊。藍天碧海，漁船遊艇，尤其傍晚時分，滿天湛紅，也是北台灣難得一見的濱海風情。

淡江大橋

淡江大橋將是一座跨越淡水河河口的雙層橋樑，為台灣第一座鐵路軌道和道路共構的雙層橋樑。1980 年代末提出興建計畫，全長 12 公里，包含主橋 900 公尺及兩端聯絡道，屬於雙層橋樑，橋面總寬 44 公尺，橋高 20 公尺，下層橋樑，設計車輛行駛時速 100 公里，上層橋樑，中央規劃為 8 公尺寬的輕軌路軌，耗資新臺幣 153 億元。將於 2016 年動工，並計於 2020 年完工通車。預計完工後，可以舒緩關渡大橋的交通流量，並且帶動淡海新市鎮的開發。

尋奇對話

Q 從高處看淡水，確實別有一番風情。整個城鎮看起來很休閒，也很幸福！

A 最近台灣也有人從空中拍了一部紀錄片《看見台灣》，很新奇，也很令人感動。台灣真的有如 400 年前航行經過此地的葡萄牙水手的驚呼「Ilha Formosa!」（美麗之島）那樣。

Q 不過，聽說這部紀錄片也讓許多台灣人警覺到過度開發的後果……。

A 是啊！有節制的開發是必要的。未來的「淡江大橋」也是花了 20 多年的討論才順利通過的……。

Q 橋應該是優先且必要的項目。屆時淡水可能更加繁榮了！

A 我們希望它是有計畫的成長，不然「人滿為患」，古有明訓！

Q 夏天這裡很熱鬧，冬天應該很少人來吧？

A 夏秋兩季這裡很熱鬧，幾乎像極了國外的渡假聖地，有音樂會，有藝術市集等等，最重要的是天天可以欣賞日落，看霞光滿天。春冬多雨又寒冷，旅客自然少了許多。不過，當地的旅遊業者也有許多吸引遊客的配套措施。

Q 聽說這裡的海鮮很地道？

A 淡水究竟還是漁港，自然有許多新鮮的漁貨，那就看你敢不敢嘗試哩！

Tamsui
11

紅樹林

到了捷運「紅樹林站」一眼就可看到綠油油的一片紅樹林。
1986年它被劃為「淡水紅樹林生態保護區」，總面積為76公頃，
是淡水河從上游所堆積而成的海岸沙洲沼澤區，也是台灣面積
最大，全世界緯度最北的紅樹林自然分佈地點。這些生命旺盛
的水生植物因枝枝泛紅而得名。紅樹林這種濕地生態系統對人
類有很高的利用價值，包括保護堤岸、河岸、海岸，供應魚苗
資源，提供野生物棲息及繁殖場所，海岸景觀林，休閒旅遊場
所及提供薪材，也有「水中森林」及「候鳥樂園」之稱。

白鷺鷥

白鷺鷥是台灣很普遍的留鳥，它們經常活動於水澤、湖泊附近，以魚類、蛙類及昆蟲為主食。喜歡群體居住，淡水紅樹林就是它們最大的家，估計有數百隻棲息於此。每到傍晚時分，三五成群翱翔歸巢，吵嚷聲此起彼落。白鷺鷥體色潔白，含有聖潔之意。步伐穩重、氣質高貴，活動敏捷、飛行姿態優美。傳說中，白鷺鷥棲居福地，在有水稻的地方，就有白鷺鷥前來啄蟲，保護農作。

水筆仔

竹圍至淡水之間的紅樹林是全然由「水筆仔」所組成的樹林。其得名係因為幼苗像筆一樣懸掛在樹枝上，長約 10 到 15 公分。這些樹的果實仍在母樹上時，胚即自種子長出，形成胎生苗。幼苗垂掛在枝條上，可自母株吸取養份。當幼苗脫離母株時，有些可插入泥中，側根再長出，再長成幼樹。有些幼苗縱使沒有順利插入泥中，能隨波逐流，再定著在適當地點。在鹽度高、土質鬆軟、缺氧及水中含氯量高的環境下，胎生現象正是最有利的適應方法。

生態步道

「淡水紅樹林生態步道」入口就在捷運紅樹林站旁，這段步道由實木搭建，在紅樹林生態區中蜿蜒而行。長度短短不到 1 公里，沿途便可眺望觀音山景、欣賞淡水河風光及濕地多元動植物生態。 站在步道上可以近距離觀看、甚至觸摸水筆仔。招潮蟹就在腳下肆意「橫行」，白鷺鷥在不遠處緊盯水面追蹤獵物。除了美麗的風景、有趣的潮間帶生物，這裡還有許多讓愛鳥人士趨之若鶩的野鳥。也是溼地生態實地教學好去處與賞鳥好地點。每年 9 月至隔年 5 月為候鳥過境的季節，是賞鳥的好時機。

尋奇對話

Q 台灣人好像很喜歡白鷺鷥？往淡水的公路旁也有它們飛舞的圖案！

A 是的。有一首耳熟能詳的台灣童謠，歌詞是：「白鷺鷥車畚箕，車到溪仔墘，跌一倒，拾到一先錢。」指小孩子一無所有，希望化成白鷺鷥，能碰到好運氣，在路上撿到錢！

Q 淡水的紅樹林會有許多候鳥經過嗎？

A 據野鳥協會統計，大約會有10餘種。不過數量應不會太多，因為太靠近市區，人聲鼎沸，覓食也不易。不過體型較小的候鳥比較常見，尤其在關渡平原，那裡還築了好幾間觀鳥小屋，可就近觀看。

Q 關渡平原應該就屬於所謂的「濕地」了？它有受到保護嗎？

A 應該算是有。政府將它列為「低度開發區」。現在台灣人越來越重視保留「濕地」，也更積極地加以利用，譬如，規劃成保育區、生態教育園區，或者親子休閒區等等。

Q 聽說關渡平原以前還是一片大沼澤，唭哩岸以前還是個河港？

A 事實上，台北盆地以前有許多地區也是沼澤地。目前有些地方的地面只比海平面高出一點而已！所以經常會鬧水災。台北捷運以前也被大水淹過，停駛了好幾個星期。

Q 所以台北是個「水鄉澤國」？

A 治水一直都是台灣很重要的施政，但我們現在很喜歡親水！

淡水小吃

Tamsui
12

淡水是的傳統的漁港，過去更是台灣重要的通商口岸，因此物資豐富，海產類更是這裡的一大特色，加上交通、歷史與地方發展，孕育出豐富而多元的飲食文化。淡水老街歷史悠久，也發展出多樣的飲食風貌。淡水的小吃百百種，但最有名的有魚丸、魚酥、「鐵蛋」、「阿給」。這些有名的小吃大部分是就地取材，反映基層民眾的基本飲食需求，也烙印著許多文化融合及社會嚮往。從普羅市井小吃到海鮮大餐、異國料理等。其中「阿給」及「鐵蛋」更是淡水老街最具特殊風味的小吃。

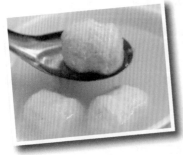

魚丸

淡水早期是漁港,漁獲量大,以致於供過於求,捕來的漁獲除了在市場販賣外,更延伸出許多附加產品,如魚乾、魚酥、魚丸等。魚丸是將中、大型魚肉(鯊魚或鬼頭刀)磨成魚漿後,加少許太白粉和水調和,製成魚丸外皮,中間則包入特殊的豬肉燥。煮湯食用,香味濃郁。其實全世界各地都有「魚丸」,口味的差異多來自魚種及手工,還有配料。

鐵蛋

早期在淡水渡船頭的一位麵攤子老闆娘阿哖婆,將賣不出去的滷蛋回鍋再滷,結果,滷蛋變得又黑又小,像鐵一樣,有些顧客好奇,就買來試吃,覺得又香又耐嚼,於是聲名漸漸遠播,「鐵蛋」因而得名,習稱「阿婆鐵蛋」,成了淡水有名的特色小吃。鐵蛋的製作過程很費工費時,每天必須用醬油及五香配方調配的滷料,經過幾個小時的滷製,然後用風乾,反覆持續幾天才能完成。

傳統糕餅

淡水有許多老字號傳統糕餅舖,傳統古早餅,口味眾多,多遵行古法精製、每一個糕餅都保留著令人懷念的古早味,每一口都能讓遊客感受到回味不盡的鄉土味,是淡水重要的傳統美食。1984 年其中一家新勝發,還曾獲得日本糕餅比賽博覽會的金賞獎!台灣婚習俗中,女方會訂做許多「禮餅」分贈親友,為了不要「失禮」,大多會精挑細選風味及口感一流的淡水喜餅。

魚丸博物館

充分利用淡水漁港龐大的漁獲，
1963 年登峰公司創新開發出淡
水魚酥，目的是提供民眾一份
佐餐品，之後成了休閒食品、
觀光禮品。2004 年，店老闆
在淡水老街上開設「魚丸博物
館」供民眾參觀，它是全台
第一座以魚丸為主題的博物

館，也能安排 DIY 參訪的「觀光工廠」。博物館佔地約
70 餘坪，共有三層樓，一樓為產品販售區，二樓為展示廳，陳列許多
捕魚的古董器皿及歷史照片圖說，還展示一支 1884 年中法滬尾之役法
國海軍陸戰隊所使用的制式步槍（Fusil Gras M80 1874）原品。

阿給

「阿給」是日文「油豆腐」（あ
ぶらあげ／阿布拉給）發音的
直接簡化音譯。做法是將四方
形豆腐中間挖空，然後填入冬
粉，再以魚漿封口後，加以蒸
熟，食用時淋上甜辣醬，再加
上魚丸湯或大骨湯汁，即是
讓人食指大動的阿給美食。「阿給」應是
淡水口味最獨特的地方小吃。1965 年由楊鄭錦文女士所發明，起初是
因不想浪費賣剩的食材，而想出的特殊料理方式。創始店位於淡水鎮真
理街上，專作學生的早餐與午餐。

尋奇對話

Q 很多人來台灣觀光旅遊很可能就是衝著想享用這裡的美食？

A 台灣的美食在世界排名數一數二，可以跟它媲美的大概只有地中海菜及日本料理。此外，在台灣，人們幾乎可以吃到中國各地的佳餚。在香港及中國大陸就沒有這種多樣性。

Q 美食和小吃有何不同？

A 美食是大宴，通常會有 10 到 12 道菜餚。小吃通常只有單味，傳統市場邊都吃得到。尤其在夜市，它更是以提供各式各樣的小吃為賣點。

Q 聽說現在台灣政要宴請國外貴賓，甚至在國宴上，也會安排推薦台灣地方小吃？

A 對啊！因為有些小吃還真的在其他地區，或國家根本吃不到！是真正的「台味」！

Q 台灣小吃有幾種？那裡吃得到？

A 應該沒有人統計過，即便同樣一款，各地的口味、配料也不同！要吃小吃一定要到夜市。也有一些餐廳開始專賣台式的小吃。但並不是所有的小吃都能搬得上檯面的！

Q 所以，來台灣觀光旅遊一定要到夜市吃小吃！

A 不過，還是要提醒你，夜市小吃的衛生條件、服務及用餐品質一向不夠好，你心裡要先有準備！

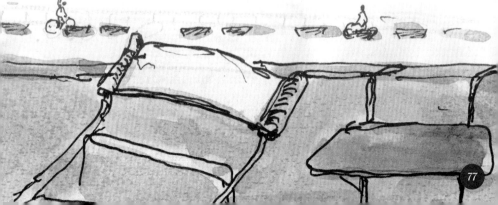

Tamsui
13

淡水藝文

淡水既是古代漢人移入的北方門戶，又是列強爭奪的據點，還一度淪為日本殖民地達半世紀之久，早年是海峽兩岸及國際通商的要埠，所以歷史古蹟、文物豐富。加上地勢優良，山海交接，河運通達，所以人文薈萃，不僅城鎮生命力旺盛，文藝風氣亦深烙民心。古代迄今定期有民間自發藝文活動，如廟會迎神、樂團劇社。現今則規劃有淡水踩街藝術節、亞洲藝術村、雲門舞集淡水園區等。淡水藝文活動的最大資產在於，它擁有人文厚度、歷史感、國際觀，加上美麗的景致、旺盛的商業活動及便捷的交通。

一滴水紀念館

「一滴水紀念館」位於滬尾砲台左側。該棟日式建築原是日本福井縣的古民宅，已有近百年的歷史，是日本作家水上勉的父親手所建的舊居，特別援引水上勉說的「一滴水脈有無限可能」做命名。1995 年阪神大地震時，這棟古民宅未遭毀壞。屋主為了讓同鄉災民有個懷想的地方，便把房子捐出。1999 年台灣發生 921 大地震，日本阪神地震的受災者來台協助災區重建工作，決定把這棟日式古民宅贈與台灣。經過一年多的努力，在來自日本及台灣志工 1300 人的攜手合作下，於 2009 年 8 月 16 日原封不動的組裝完成，並於 2011 年 3 月 29 日開館。

淡水大拜拜

「大拜拜」之意為：寺廟謝神或建醮等重大慶典時所舉行的儀式，及宴請流水席。所以會有迎神活動、親友相聚，大吃大喝的。早期先民渡海來台灣拓墾，因為水土不服、瘟疫、天災或戰亂等因素，移民會奉請家鄉守護神隨同來台灣，求消災解厄保平安。如今，拜拜已跨越宗教信仰的範疇，成為台灣人民生活文化不可或缺的一部份。「淡水大拜拜」是淡水祖師廟的慶祝活動，於每年舊曆五月初六（西曆六月中旬）舉行祭典，每年都萬人空巷，都得進行一整天的交通管制。

淡水藝術節

淡水國際環境藝術節踩街嘉年華，自 2008 年起，每年 10 月在淡水市區舉行。2013 年以「世界萬花筒」為主題，充分表現出淡水多元文化與異國風情，共有 50 個隊伍、超過 1500 人，以創意、熱情走踏淡水街道。這項藝術嘉年華的活動是由多位藝術家及社區居民通力合作和參與，將淡水的歷史、傳說、風土人文、及當代日常生活，化為創作素材。透過「藝術踩街」與「環境戲劇」演出，以呈現四百年來淡水的獨特藝術饗宴。近來也結合國際藝術團體的邀訪，使這項活動更具多元及吸引力。

尋奇對話

Q 「一滴水紀念館」的故事很感人，台灣與日本的關係真的很特殊，很密切！

A 台日民間交流一向很密切，觀光旅遊及商務貿易有來有往，而且十分興盛。透過眼見為憑及交流就更能瞭解對方！

Q 「雲門舞集」是國際最知名的台灣表演藝團，將來它的「淡水園區」應更可帶動此地的藝文活動及曝光率！

A 聽說當初是雲門主動選上淡水的！屆時整個園區會對外開放，包括供民眾參訪及安排表演工作坊。

Q 西方人或其他民族會用牛或羊當犧牲，台灣地區為何會選中豬當牲品呢？

A 台灣地區過去家家戶戶都會養豬。中文「家」字就說明一切：養了豬才能成家。這裡比較少人養牛羊，而且耕種的農民比較疼惜牛的辛勞，所以祭拜都用大豬公。

Q 聽說台灣也有養豬公這個專門行業，甚至還比賽誰養得最大隻？

A 這是一種榮譽，也是對神明的最大敬意。史上最重的豬公達 1683 台斤（合 1010 公斤）。那是要花好幾年細心照料才有可能。人們會宴客（通常都是流水席），也會分贈豬肉給親友。

Q 將來如果能將迎神、拜拜及藝術嘉年華會結合在一起，應該是蠻不錯的點子！

A 啊呀！你很適合當我們的文化部長！

淡江大學

Tamsui
14

一所沒有宗教、企業背景的大學，以校風開放著稱。也是一所「沒有圍牆的學校」。創辦之初，淡水居民出地捐輸功不可沒。校園與居民共享共營是一大特色。1950 張鳴（驚聲）、張建邦父子發想所創，初期為英語專科學校， 1958 年改制為文理學院，1980 年正名為淡江大學。迄今擁有淡水、台北、蘭陽、網路等 4 個校園之綜合型大學，有 8 個學院，27000 餘名學生，2100 餘位專兼任教職員工，及 24 萬多名校友，是台灣最具規模且功能完備的高等教育學府之一。《Cheers》雜誌在《2015最佳大學指南》發佈 2015 年 2000 大企業最愛大學生調查，淡大第 18 度蟬聯私立大學之冠。

宮燈教室

淡江大學的風景及建物雅致，口碑相傳，揚名中外。早年還是電視連續劇及電影取景的熱點。當中最著名的首推興建於1954年的「宮燈教室」。它依山丘斜坡興建，雙排對稱的仿唐朝傳統建築，碧瓦紅牆，扶搖直上；前後綠地，窗明几淨。中央一長排宮燈，有9根仿古華表，18條蟠龍，上方掛起兩盞宮燈。每當華燈初上，與一輪火紅夕陽相互輝映。其設計出自淡大建築系首任系主任馬惕乾之手，於1955年全部建成啟用，迄今已育逾半世紀！

海事博物館

淡江大學海事博物館為一獨棟2134平方公尺的船型建築，前身為「商船學館」，是淡江大學專門培育航海、輪機科技人才的搖籃。由長榮集團總裁張榮發先生捐資興建，並捐贈各項有關航海、輪機之教學設備。

後因國家教育政策的變更，奉令停止招收航海、輪機的學生，俟1989年送走最後一屆學生後，擘劃興建為全國首座「海事博物館」，展示古今中外各類的船艦模型。當時董事長林添福亦捐贈私人收藏的50餘艘全球知名船艦模型。1990年6月開館，免費供各界參觀。

蛋捲廣場

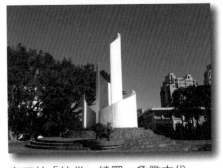

位於淡大校園中心點的「蛋捲廣場」，原為一方正有中庭的二層樓綜合教室。1986 年拆除改成綠地廣場，中央由建築師林貴榮校友設計一座建物，有四片「竹卷」繞圈，象徵古代的簡冊，故命名「書卷廣場」，因酷似蛋捲，遂有了「蛋捲廣場」之別名。從上俯視，像馬達中的轉軸，生生不息。雪白瀟灑的弧型造形，不論藍天、黃昏或夜晚，都呈現出不同的迷人景致。目前它是淡大許多社團聚會及大型活動舉辦的地方，也是每位淡江人拍照、懷念的景點。

淡大校歌

作詞 / 鄒魯　作曲 / 呂泉生

浩浩淡江 萬里通航 新舊思想 輸來相將

博學審問 明辨篤行 自成機杼 用為世匡

學戒驕固 技守專長 樸實剛毅 大用是彰

彼時代之菁莪兮 國家之貞良

（願）乾乾惕厲兮 莫辜負大好之時光

尋奇對話

Q 淡大畢業生連續 17 年獲企業界肯定，排名私校第一，全國第八！淡江畢業的學生還真的了不起！

A 主要原因是淡江大學是一所老字號的綜合型大學，做出了品牌。另外學風自由，學校治理相當前瞻及靈活。很早就提出三化：國際化、資訊化、未來化。

Q 擁有 24 萬名校友，應該是很大的社會資源。

A 換算一下，每 100 個台灣人就有一個是淡大畢業的！這還不包括他（她）們的家庭，他（她）們肯定都是淡江大學的代言人。這裡還出現過三代都是淡大畢業的！

Q 淡江大學已創立 60 餘年，一提到淡水都會想到淡江大學？

A 是的！淡江大學就屬於淡水。淡水基本上就是一座大學城。除了淡大，還有真理大學、聖約翰科技大學、台北海洋技術學院分校，及關渡基督學院等共 5 所高等學院。

Q　淡江大學畢業校友最懷念學校的地方是什麼？

A　四時變化的校園風景啊！尤其是古色古香的宮燈教室。每年3月校友回娘家日，校友們都會指定到宮燈教室裡重溫舊夢！

Q　淡江大學是民歌的發源地，音樂風氣應該很盛吧？

A　這裡沒有音樂系，但有一個很不錯的音樂廳。校園音樂活動一直很興盛，也養育不少知名歌手。藝文界及影視圈的校友也很多。反正，這裡很美，所以學生們都很懂得欣賞美！

河岸自行車道

Tamsui 15

淡水至紅樹林自行車道，沿河濱架設，車道長約 2.5 公里。可騎上公路延伸至淡海的漁人碼頭，亦可上關渡大橋，轉八里左岸自行車道風景區，直達十三行博物館。自行車道內只有行人及腳踏車才能進入，是最安全又愜意的單車之旅。自行車道一邊是綿延無際的海岸風光與濃密紅樹林水筆仔，一邊是疾駛如風的捷運，行在其中，山光水色盡收眼底。自行車道沿線設置觀景平台，不時可見白鷺鷥飛翔、招潮蟹橫行、彈塗魚的身影，可體驗淡水河岸好風光及對岸蒼鬱的觀音山、野鳥群飛、夕陽落日等美景。

假日單車

台北市政府自 2002 年開始規劃全市河濱自行車道，完成環繞台北市河濱，包括淡水河、基隆河、景美溪及新店溪等四大系統，南起景美、東自內湖，沿著河岸二側向下游延伸至關渡濕地，形成總長約 111 公里的河濱自行車道網絡。並根據各河川沿線不同的景觀及特色，將河濱自行車道規劃為「關渡、金色水岸、八里左岸自行車道」等不同休閒主題的自行車道。沿線豐富的自然、人文、古蹟等美麗景觀，提供給民眾假日的休閒好去處。完工以來，頗獲好評，假日騎單車幾乎蔚為台灣的國民運動！

河岸馳騁

台灣號稱自行車王國，捷安特（Giant）、美利達（Merida）早已是世界自行車十大暢銷品牌。台灣每年生產超過 440 萬輛自行車。許多國際名牌自行車也多委託台灣工廠生產。有 270 萬人以單車做為運動項目，70 萬人以單車為交通工具。單車環島更是最近最夯的運動項目。目前全台已建構完成 40 條自行車道，約有 1180 公里。其中大多沿河岸開闢。淡水到新店河岸自行車道全長 60 公里，假日騎乘人口更如過江之鯽。一方面運動休閒，另一方面親近河水，達到生態休閒旅遊的目的。

微笑單車（U-bike）

由台北市政府委託捷安特自行車建置和營運，並以「YouBike 微笑單車」作為對外的服務品牌（以 U-bike 為標誌）。它採無人化自助式服務，於 2009 年 3 月開始示範營運，最後在 2012 年 11 月正式啟用。YouBike 目前已經發出 13 萬張會員卡，累計的租賃次數超過 100 萬人次。截至 2014 年 2 月，YouBike 在台北市共有 158 個租賃站點。這項創舉開辦之初虧損連連，後來改成前半小時免費及廣設據點，租乘才蔚為風氣，成了台北市一項特殊景觀。人們也可以在淡水自行車道上看到它的蹤影。

尋奇對話

Q 聽說你曾去單車環島過，總共花了幾天？

A 全程 900 餘公里，我們一共花了 9 天。不過專業型的可以 7 天，甚至 5 天，還有人挑戰 3 天！

Q 台灣的年輕人為什麼特別喜歡單車環島？

A 因為相當方便，這也是親近自己的土地的一種方式。網路 也鼓吹愛台灣的三項運動：單車環島、登玉山、泳渡日月潭。

Q 聽說很多企業及單位為提醒員工多運動，還會舉辦企業團 體自行車旅遊？

A 最有名的應該是捷安特自行車製造場老闆劉金標老先生， 70 多歲的他還帶領高級主管單車環島好幾次！

Q 台北市的「微笑單車」相當有名，連《國際旅遊雜誌》
（*Global Traveler*）都曾專文推介。

A 2007 年法國巴黎街頭最早推出公共自助自行車（Vélib'），
帶起了一股自行車風潮，世界其他主要城市也紛紛跟進。
台北市的「微笑單車」租借系統便是取法巴黎，並將刷卡
系統結合捷運悠遊卡。

Q 外國觀光客也可以借用嗎？

A 當然可以！只要買一張捷運悠遊卡，在街頭的服務柱上自
行辦妥登記就可以了。

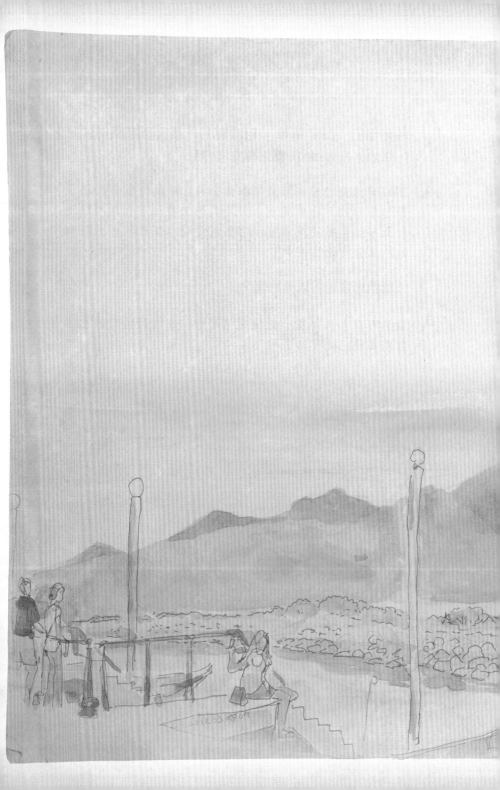

Let's Talk about Tamsui

Tamsui
01

歷史上的淡水

Tamsui in History

Tamsui, a village located next to a mountain and a river, has a unique charm. For a hundred years and through the ages, it has been the final home of numerous immigrants from the South China Sea and Mainland China. It is full of the stories and history of its residents. A panorama of Tamsui taken from Guan Yin Moutain reveals the full charisma of this village. A peaceful mind and sense of ease permeate Tamsui with its ancient fortress (which is over 300 years old), old streets, temples, exotic houses, beautiful scenery, bike paths and even the modern MRT trains rushing by.

Where is Tamsui Located?

Tamsui is located in the northwest of the Taipei basin and by the Taiwan Strait, which is at the estuary of the Tamsui River. It is east of the city of Taipei, north of Sanchi and south of Pali, with the Tamsui River in between. Tamsui is situated among the mountains of the Tatun volcanic group, also known as Five-Tiger Hill. The only narrow plain is located in the south, and it goes along the Tamsui River.

The New Eight Sceneries in Tamsui

1. The Panorama in Buding
2. The View of Tatun Volcano
3. The Beach at Shalun
4. The Tamsui River Bank
5. The Mangrove by Guandu Bridge (Mangrove and Guandu Bridge)
6. The Glow at the Tamsui River Estuary
7. Guan Yin Mountain by the River
8. The Nostalgia of Old Street

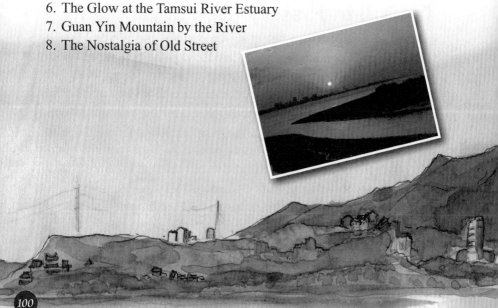

How was Tamsui Named?

According to the research of historian Chen Zong-Ren, in ancient times Tamsui was where Chinese ships got fresh water and supplies. So Tamsui was named after its literal function. In the 17th century, Taiwan was the hub of East Asian international trade, which made it very desirable to western colonial powers. As the crucial port in northern Taiwan, Tamsui was very important. The name Tamsui has been found on many maps and literature compiled by westerners, although there have been several spellings, such as Tanchi or Tamchuy for the Spanish and Tamsy for the Dutch. They all derived from Tamsui, which is why it is the most commonly accepted form. Tamsui is associated with fresh water, particularly the Tamsui River near the mouth of the sea.

Hobe Defined

There are four parts related to the name origin of Hobe, which is the ancient name of Tamsui. They were related to water, fishery and the sound transfer from aboriginal language. According to The Textual Research on the Origin of Hobe, a book by historian Zhang Jian-Long, Hobe derived its name from the tribe of aborigines that originally lived there. There was a tribe called Hobe west of the Tamsui battalion marked on The Ancient Map of Taiwan and Penghu, which was drawn in the times of the Yongzheng Emperor of the Qing Dynasty.

Dialogue

Q **Tamsui in English literally means "fresh water." What an interesting name.**

A There is more than one name. Some say that the Han people who lived and worked on boats found fresh water in Tamsui, which is why the name they chose literally means fresh water. Another name that has been used is Hobe, which was said to be the name of the aboriginal tribe who originally lived there.

Q **What were the powers that followed the Han people?**

A The earliest was the Dutch, followed by the Spanish, French, British and finally, the Japanese. The Qing Dynasty was forced to cede Taiwan to Japan after being defeated in war. Taiwan was then under Japanese control for 50 years (until 1945).

Q The current society in Tamsui is Han Chinese, as is most of the people. When did they start immigrating there?

A Tamsui is situated fairly close to Mainland China, with the nearest point being only about 130 kilometers away. People from the coast of the mainland started immigrating there illegally in great numbers around the 18th century. At the time, Tamsui was the only port and gateway to northern Taiwan. Not until 1885 did the Qing Dynasty incorporate Taiwan into its territory and set up a provincial capital.

Q Did a Hollywood movie studio film a movie called The Sand Pebbles, starring Steve McQueen, there?

A Yes. It was shot in Tamsui in 1965. The plot was that an American ship patrolling the Yangze River in 1926 got involved in the Chinese civil war.

Q So are there numerous historical sites in Tamsui?

A Yes, more than any other city in Taiwan. There is a lot of history and cultural activities. Tamsui is a very important tourist and resort destination in northern Taiwan.

Keywords

01. unique: a. 獨特的、獨一無二
02. charm: n. 迷人、魅力；charming: a. 有魅力的
03. panorama [ˌpænəˈræmə]: n. 全景、全貌
04. exotic [ɛgˈzɑtɪk]: a. 異國情調、奇特的
05. Han people: n. 漢人
06. aborigine [æbəˈrɪdʒən]: n. 原住民；
    aboriginal [ˌæbəˈrɪdʒən!]: a. 原住民的
07. tribe [traɪb]: n. 部落、種族
08. cede [sid]: v. 割讓、讓與、交出
09. immigrate [ˈɪməˌgret]: v. 遷移、遷入
10. incorporate [ɪnˈkɔrpəˌret]: v. 把……合併、使併入
11. the Yangtze River: n. 長江
12. scenario [sɪˈnɛrɪˌo]: n. 情節、劇本
13. resort [rɪˈzɔrt]: n. 常去的休閒度假之處、名勝
15. plain [plen]: n. 平原、曠野 a. 簡樸的、樸素的、不攙雜的
16. nostalgia [nɑsˈtældʒɪə]: n. 鄉愁、 懷舊之情
17. textual research: n. 考證
18. sound transfer: n. 音轉

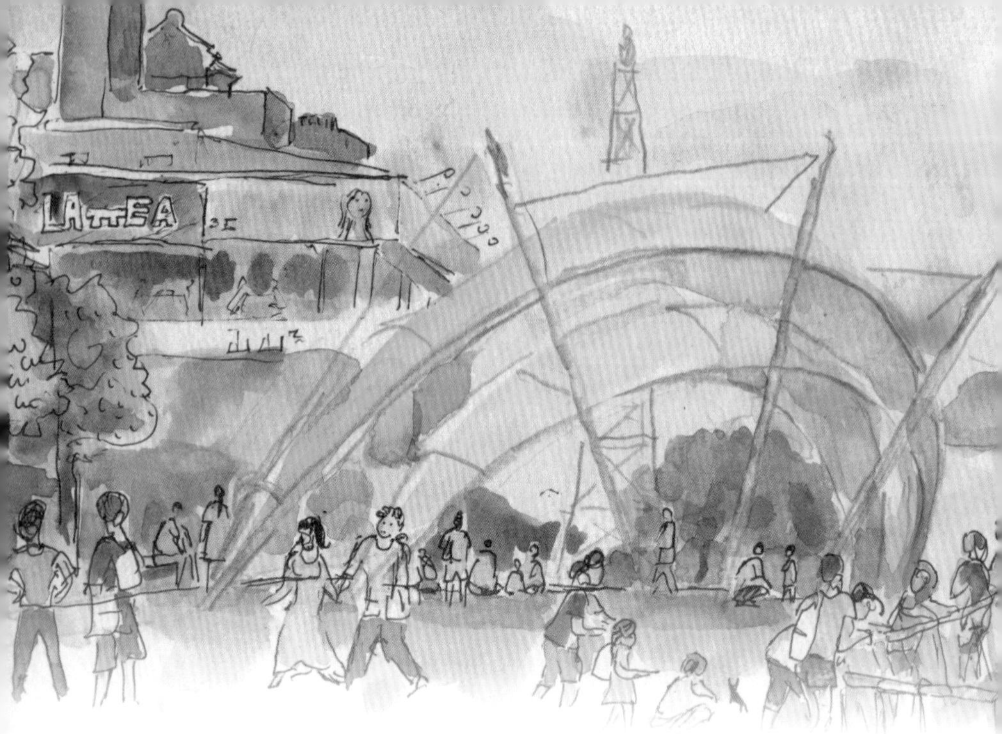

Tamsui
02

渡船頭

THE FERRY

The Tamsui ferry system was the largest gateway to northern Taiwan for Han immigrants. It played a large role in shipping as well. It would be hard to imagine all the hustle and bustle of sailboats filing into the ferry terminal two hundred years ago. While Taiwan was under Japanese control, Keelung took over Tamsui as a major hub of sea transportation. But it wasn't until 1982 that the ferry system became truly obsolete when the Guandu Bridge was opened. The only remaining ferry transports are the ones between Tamsui and Pali. These leisurely blue-hulled ships paint a pretty picture for those who like to watch them scuttle back and forth. In 2004 floating piers were erected and the so-called "Blue Highway" was opened to facilitate tourism and sightseeing. Nowadays there's a Fisherman's Wharf and many other attractions with modern style for tourists and sightseers.

The Tamsui Ferry System

The Tamsui ferry system was the main gateway to northern Taiwan in ancient times. Their sails could constantly be seen traveling to and fro. The modern piers were completed in July 2004. These floating piers facilitate tour boats and boost the flow of traffic. Boats travel around scenic spots such as Fisherman's Wharf and Pali, broadening recreation opportunities and making sightseeing of the land along the river possible. In the evening, light from the setting sun floods the river and Guan Yin Mountain, lending the background a quality not unlike a landscape painting. The Guandu Bridge can be seen in the distance when taking the ferry down the Tamsui River. The river glitters with a golden color at nightfall and reflects the moonlight at night. It is soothing indeed.

Blue Highway
(or waterway transportation)

The purpose of the Blue Highway is to develop tourism and river transport on the Tamsui and Keelung Rivers. Since opening to traffic, eight inland ship routes have been established and passenger capacity has increased to over one million. The guided tours are rich in history and ecology. The North Taiwan Blue Highway and North Coast Blue Highway have greatly increased tourism, and the area offers comprehensive leisure activities. Japanese language guided tours have been arranged with the hope of increasing tourism from Japan. A direct route to Fuzhou in China is also planned to encourage tourists from the mainland.

The Sunset at Tamsui

Tamsui, located at the junction of a river and a mountain, has a spectacular sunset that reflects beautifully on the water. It has inspired poets, painters and photographers. Especially in the crisp autumn, the rays of the evening sunlight flood into town and casts itself on all passers-by.

The Wanderers at Tamsui

Lyricist / Chen Ming-Zhang   Melodist / China Blue

Let's enjoy the party freely and widely.

Liquor up! Cheer up! Bottoms up!

Our hand organ and guitar are not our self-amusing but they are our livelihood.

I get lovesick every time I think of the one I love.

Alcohol loosens me up and lifts my spirits up. Let bygones be bygones.

Save a place in your heart for your loved one. Start a brand new life in a place far from home.

It's not superficial brilliance, but poverty that motivates us.

Whether the weather is good or bad, we will sing nostalgic love songs.

Tears and laughter, separation and reunion are part of life just as the moon has different phases.

Seize the day. Focus on the present. Let's chant and dance.

Let's enjoy the party freely and wildly.

Liquor up! Cheer up! Bottoms up! (X 3)

Dialogue

Q **It takes only 35 minutes to reach Tamsui. It's very convenient and there's lots of nice scenery to see along the way.**

A The Taipei Metro system is getting more convenient and well-connected. What an attraction for tourists. On holidays and weekends, Tamsui is packed.

Q **Besides the Taipei Metro, there are other convenient ways to get to Tamsui.**

A You can get to Tamsui by either land or sea. However, the Metro is the most convenient for people who don't drive. Opened to traffic in 1997, it was built on the foundation of the Japanese-built Tamsui train line that ran from 1901 to 1988.

Q **Could we also take a boat to Tamsui?**

A Sure. Since 2005, boats have been able to go from Dadaocheng in the historic section of Taipei City to Tamsui, the Fisherman's Wharf, or even the estuary. There is also "The Queen of the Great River" cruise, which uses a ship that's designed to look like an old American steamboat and, which will take you on a sightseeing tour of the Tamsui River.

Q **It seems like a lot of people live in Tamsui, and many of them are young.**

A Tamsui has an official registered population of around 150, 000. The reality is that there's often more than that. The five universities there add a large "floating" population. Being near Taipei and having convenient transportation and low housing prices make it a top choice for young couples.

Q **Do a lot of people visit Tamsui?**

A Yes. The scenic spots alone attract up to 5 million people per year. Since ancient times, Tamsui has been renowned for tourism. And the sunset at Tamsui is one of the "Eight Sceneries of Taiwan."

Keywords

01. ferry [`fɛrɪ]: n. 渡輪，聯運船，擺渡船
02. downfall [`daʊnˌfɔl]: n. 沒落
03. shuttle [`ʃʌt!]: n. 短程穿梭運行
04. floating pier [pɪr]: n. 浮動式碼頭
05. motor-powered: a. 由馬達、電動機所產生動力的
06. Shangri-la [`ʃæŋgrɪ`lɑ]: n. 幻想的世外桃源
07. well-connected: a. (指捷運網絡) 良好連接的
08. packed [pækt]: a. 塞得滿滿的，擁擠的
09. boat restaurant: n. 餐船
10. populous [`pɑpjələs]: a. 人口眾多的，人口稠密的
11. floating [`flotɪŋ] population: n. 流動人口
12. the top choice for: n. 首選
13. renowned [rɪ`naʊnd]: a. 有名的；有聲譽的
14. spectacular [spɛk`tækjələ˞]: a. 壯觀的；壯麗的
15. crisp autumn: 秋高氣爽

16. breath-taking: a. 嘆為觀止

17. inspire [ɪn`spaɪr]: v. 賦予……靈感，給……以啟示

18. superficial [`supɚ`fɪʃəl] brilliance: 虛有其表

19. poverty [`pɑvɚtɪ]: n. 貧窮

20. gateway [`get͵we]: n. 途徑、方法、門戶、通道

21. facilitate [fə`sɪlə͵tet]: v. 促進；幫助

22. gigantic [dʒaɪ`gæntɪk]: a. 巨大的，龐大的

23. portray [por`tre]: v. 畫（人物，風景等）、（用語言）描寫

24. soothing [`suðɪŋ]: a. 慰藉的、使人寬心的

25. direct route [rut]: n. 直航

26. knowledgeable [`nɑlɪdʒəb!]: a. 知性、有知識的、博學的

27. ecology [ɪ`kɑlədʒɪ]: n. 生態

28. passenger [`pæsndʒɚ] capacity [kə`pæsətɪ]: n. 載客量

Tamsui
03

紅毛城

FORT SAN DOMINGO (The Red Castle)

Fort San Domingo was built by the Spanish when they occupied the north of Taiwan in 1628. In 1644, it was renovated by the Dutch. The locals at the time nicknamed the Dutch "the red-haired people, " and as a result the fortress was named Red Castle. In 1661, Koxinga repelled the Dutch and managed Taiwan for a short time. During the Qing Dynasty the fort was renovated once again and used as a military stronghold. In 1867, the Red Castle was leased by the British for long-term use as the British Consulate, and in 1891 a Victorian-styled residence was built behind it. Fort San Domingo was put under the trusteeship of Australia and the United States of America in 1972, during a time when British-ROC diplomatic ties were severed. Not until 1980 were the property rights passed on to the ROC. It was then that Fort San Domingo, one of the oldest working buildings in Taiwan, was made a national monument, renovated, and named Tamsui Historical Museum.

Fort San Domingo in Hobe

"… The waves came in a line, as rumbling as thunder and as dreamy as hallucinations. In a wink of time, the spectacular sunset glittered. The panorama from the pavilion went on in a grand manner with the banks, clouds, trees, sails and seabirds."

Wu Zi-Guang, who was born in Tongluo Miaoli, was a very successful candidate in the imperial provincial examinations during the Tongzhi years of the Qing Dynasty. He was highly proficient in the Confucian classics, history, and philosophy. Wu was praised as the top scholar in Taiwan before the 20th century. Qiu Feng-Jia was his disciple. In 1866, while wandering in Tamsui as he was waiting for the boat to take him to the mainland for his exam, Wu wrote Red Castle in Hobe.

The Fortress of the Dutch

The original fortress was built of wood by the Spanish, and was eventually burnt down by Chinese locals. It was rebuilt with stone, but not after long after its completion Spain decided to withdraw its troops and ordered its destruction. In May of 1644 Dutch troops began to rebuild it once again, using stone and top quality lime and bricks from as far away as Indonesia. The solid, deep foundation and vaults were very reminiscent of a Dutch fortress, which they intended to be strong and enduring. In 1662 Koxinga expelled the Dutch from southern Taiwan, and their troops retreated to Tamsui before leaving altogether. In 1863, the British leased the fortress and renovated the cannon stronghold into a consulate, residence and four cells.

The British Consular Residence

The British consular residence is made of bricks in a Colonial Style. It is characterized by a veranda with arched corridor to avoid the tropical heat of summer, a slanted roof designed by an architect hired by the British consul, red bricks, and the work of craftsmen from Fujian and Xiamen. In the residence, the west side was built with a living room and study, the east side with a dining room and kitchen, and in the back is a laundry room and servant's quarters. There are three big bedrooms and a storeroom built on the second floor. The green area, all around the residence, was developed into rosary. Afternoon tea was generally enjoyed under the veranda. The refined design and exquisite materials embody the sensibilities of a British consular residence, a rare remnant of Western-style colonial-era buildings in East Asia.

Dialogue

Q **Were the British also considered red-haired in the eyes of the Chinese?**

A Yes, they were. Caucasians in general were thought to have red or brown hair, and as a result foreigners were always nicknamed "the red-haired." The nearly 400-year history of Fort San Domingo — which involved Spain, the Netherlands, Koxinga of the Ming Dynasty, the Qing Dynasty, the UK, Japan, the USA and Australia — reflects the history of Taiwan itself.

Q **How many British consulates were built by the British in Taiwan?**

A There were three in total, located in Kaohsiung, Anping and Tamsui. The one in Tamsui was the most recently built, the largest in scale, the best maintained, and the most scenic. All and all, the three were built with similarly Victorian style, commonly referred to as Colonial Typology.

Q Did the British consulate engage in large-scale occupational activities?

A Taiwan experienced a great leap in international trade ever since Tamsui became an international trading port, especially in the export of tea and camphor to Mainland China.

Q Did the British remain in Tamsui when the Japanese took Taiwan in 1895?

A They did. According to international law, the British government was legally entitled to stay. They didn't leave until the beginning of World War II. After it ended, they reclaimed Fort San Domingo.

Q Why did the British government wait until 1980 to return Fort San Domingo?

A They were reluctant to return it and maintained their legal right to it even when diplomatic relations were broken off in 1972. It took a lot of effort to get it back, and it's because of that effort that the fort can be visited and enjoyed today.

Keywords

01. transfer [træns`fɚ]: v. 轉交、轉移 (+ to)

02. military [`mɪləˌtɛrɪ] stronghold [`strɔŋˌhold]: n. 軍事要塞

03. lease [lis]: v. 出租 [（+out）]、租得 [（+from）]: n. 租約

04. consular [`kɑnslɚ]: a. 領事的、領事館的、領事職務的

05. residence [`rɛzədəns]: n. 住所、住宅、官邸

06. break up: v. 斷絕、關係中止

07. diplomatic [ˌdɪplə`mætɪk] tie: n. 交交關係

08. trusteeship [trʌs`tiʃɪp]: n. 託管人的地位（或職責）、託管（區域）

09. renovate [`rɛnəˌvet]: v. 整建、修理、改善

10. property [`prɑpɚtɪ] right: n. 產權、財產權

11. Koxinga: 鄭成功

12. repel [rɪ`pɛl]: v. 擊退、驅除

13. Colonial [kə`lonjəl] Typology [taɪ`pɑlədʒɪ]: n. 殖民地式建築

14. camphor [`kæmfɚ]: n. 樟腦

15. export [`ɛksport]: v. 輸出、出口

16. international [ˌɪntɚ`næʃnl] law [lɔ]: n. 國際法

17. withdrawal [wɪð`drɔəl]: v. 撤走

18. reluctant [rɪ`lʌktənt]: a. 不情願、勉強的

19. praise [prez]: n. 讚揚、稱讚

20. disciple [dɪ`saɪp!]: n. 信徒、弟子

21. lime [laɪm]: n. 石灰

22. vault [vɔlt]: n. 拱頂；穹窿

23. veranda [və`rændə]: n. 陽臺、遊廊、走廊

24. tropical [`trɑpɪk!]: a. 熱帶的、位於熱帶的

25. arched [ɑrtʃt] corridor [`kɔrɪdɚ]: n. 拱廊設計

26. servants' quarter [`kwɔrtɚ]: n. 僕人房

27. dining [`daɪnɪŋ] room: n. 餐廳

28. master [`mæstɚ] bedroom: n. 大臥室

29. storeroom: n. 貯藏室

30. rosary: n. 玫瑰園

31. refined [`rozərɪ]: a. 雅致

32. laundry [`lɔndrɪ] room: n. 洗衣間

33. reminiscent [ˌrɛmə`nɪsnt]: a. 回憶往事的、懷舊的

Tamsui
04

馬偕、教會、學校

DR. MACKAY, THE CHURCHES AND SCHOOLS

George MacKay was a missionary from Canada who founded the MacKay Hospital. The hospital still works around the clock, serving the needy. He made a great impact on Taiwan, and even has a street named after him. He spent nearly 30 years dedicated to medical care, missionary efforts, and education, and was buried in Taiwan. Leaving his hometown and arriving in Tamsui at the age of 27 in March of 1872, Dr. MacKay decided to put up in Tamsui. He established Presbyterian Churches and raised funds from the US and Canada, started a dental practice and offered medical services to the wounded soldiers of the Qing Dynasty. Despite not having a medical degree, he extracted over 20 thousand cavities. He even imported vegetable seeds such as turnips, cabbages, tomatoes, cauliflowers, and carrots.

Chapel of Presbyterian Church

The Chapel of Presbyterian Church is located on MacKay Street. The current building was renovated in 1932 and designed by George W. MacKay, the son of George Leslie MacKay. As an imitative Gothic brick work, the chapel has a square bell tower, wooden-framed ceiling and an organ that is from 1909. The chapel is the biggest of its kind in Tamsui with a capacity of 300 people. Its roof was repaired in 1986. Allegedly designed by Hong Quan and Huang A-Shu, two  prestigious craftsmen, the exterior was built with top-quality bricks formed in a regular pattern. As one of Tamsui's most distinguishable landmarks, the chapel is a favorite of artists.

Rev. George Leslie MacKay

 Born in the Ontario province of Canada, George Leslie MacKay (1844-1901), called Dr. MacKay or Pastor MacKay by the Taiwanese, was a medical doctor and Presbyterian pastor. Western historians defined the life of Dr. MacKay with his motto, "It's better to burn than to rust out." Having arrived at Kaohsiung in 1871, Dr. MacKay practiced missionary work in Tamsui, learned the Fukien language, and married a Taiwanese local. He traveled a lot and established twenty-something churches in northern and eastern Taiwan. His efforts in education included establishing Oxford College in 1882 (now called Aletheia University) and two years after that, a women's school which was a pioneer in women's education. Following in his father's footsteps, George W. MacKay founded Tamkang Senior High School. The everyday life of Dr. MacKay in Taiwan was unveiled in The Diaries of George Leslie MacKay, a work of over 700 thousand words published in three volumes.

Tamkang Senior High School

Formerly named Tamsui Middle School and Tamsui Girl's School, Tamkang Senior High School was founded by Dr. MacKay and his son. It is a rare, century-old educational institute which has witnessed the educational and cultural transition of Taiwan. Located next to both a mountain and the sea, it is known for its beautiful landscape and scenery. The campus integrates the blueprint of prestigious Western schools with the traditions of Chinese architects, forming an ideal environment for developing a well-balanced, culturally aware spirit. As the spiritual fortress of Tamkang Senior High School, the Octagonal Tower incorporates features of Chinese pagodas with the traits of Byzantine architecture. The tower, which was completed in June of 1925, was made possible by K. W. Dowie, a Canadian missionary and geometry teacher.

Dialogue

Q I caught a glimpse of MacKay Street and the statute of Dr. MacKay. Even though he's Canadian, he should be an honorary citizen of Tamsui.

A He is. Taiwan was his home for the last 30 years of his life. Tamsui was where he tirelessly established medical services, missionary efforts, and education. He was truly a blessing for Taiwan.

Q In contrast to the self-serving and often violent occupation of Taiwan by Spain, the Netherlands, France, Japan, and Britain, Dr. MacKay's Canadian approach was selfless and his good deeds brought him high esteem.

A Modern medical science was introduced to Taiwan by Dr. MacKay, who provided medical services, improved medical technology, and raised funds for hospital development. MacKay Memorial Hospital currently has four branch hospitals across the country, over three thousand beds, and over seven thousand employees. There is also the MacKay Junior College of Medicine, Nursing, and Management and the MacKay Medical College.

Q Isn't it said that Tamkang Senior High School has a beautiful campus and is also the alma mater of Jay Chou, the famous singer and songwriter?

A Yes. Tamkang Senior High School was literally the first western school established in Taiwan. Its magnificent mansion and graceful campus is a great complement to the Chinese community. It was also founded by Dr. MacKay and further developed by George William MacKay, his son. Its open academic atmosphere inspires people in both art and business. It is also the alma mater of Lee Teng-Hui, former president of the ROC.

Q **The establishment of Tamkang University had some thing to do with it, didn't it?**

A Yes, it did. Chang Ching-sheng, originally from mainland China and the founder of Tamkang University, wanted to start a university after his advanced studies in Japan. But before that he accepted an offer of employment as the principal of Tamkang Senior High School. It wasn't until 1950, after successful fundraising, that construction began on Tamkang University. Its initial location was on the site of Tamkang Senior High School!

Q **Didn't Jay Chou shoot a movie at Tamkang Senior High School?**

A Yes, he filmed his movie Secret there in 2007. Tamsui has been a favored setting for films for a long time, from The Sand Pebbles (1966) to Last Train to Tamsui (1986) to Orz Boyz (2008) and Taipei Story, the TV play (2009)

Keywords

01. prestigious [prɛs`tɪdʒɪəs]: n. 知名、有名望的

02. around the clock: 日以繼夜

03. dedicate [`dɛdə‚ket]: v. 以 ...... 奉獻，以 ...... 供奉 (+to)

04. Presbyterian [‚prɛzbə`tɪrɪən] Church: 基督長老教會

05. raise [rez] funds: v. 募款

06. carrot [`kærət]: n. 胡蘿蔔

07. cabbage [`kæbɪdʒ]: n. 甘藍菜

08. cauliflower [`kɔlə‚flauɚ]: n. 白色花椰菜；
    broccoli [`brɑkəlɪ]: n. 綠色花椰菜

09. turnip [`tɝnɪp]: n. 白蘿蔔

10. cavity [`kævətɪ]: n. 蛀牙

11. put up: v. 落腳

12. magnificent [mæg`nɪfəsənt]: a. 豪華的、華麗的

13. graceful [ˋgresfəl]: a. 優美

14. accept an offer of employment: 應聘

15. principal [ˋprɪnsəp!] : n. (中小學) 校長

16. chapel [ˋtʃæp!]: n. 禮拜堂

17. organ [ˋɔrgən]: n. 風琴

18. landmark [ˋlændˌmɑrk]: n. 地標

19. allegedly [əˋlɛdʒɪdlɪ]: adv. 據報導、據說

20. Fukien [ˋfuˋkjɛn] language: n. 閩南話

21. rare one of its kind: 罕見

22. transition [trænˋzɪʃən]: n. 變遷

23. integrate [ˋɪntəˌgret] : v. 融入

24. geometry [dʒɪˋɑmətrɪ]: n. 幾何學

25. ideal [aɪˋdiəl]: a. 理想的

觀音山

GUAN YIN MOUNTAIN

Guan Yin Mountain is located at the left bank of the Tamsui River estuary. It is 616 meters high, and its peak is named Ying Han Ling, or "Tough Summit" in English. A number of ancient temples have been found in the mountain, several of which are dedicated to Guan Yin (Guan Yin is the goddess of mercy). Guan Yin Mountain faces the Taiwan Strait on the west and overlooks Guandu on the north-east through the Tamsui River, offering marvelous views. Even when shrouded in fog, it is one of the "Eight Sceneries of Taiwan." A perfect mountain for hikers, it was named Tamswijse berch while under Dutch rule, and Parrigon Mountain by the Han people. Parrigon was the name of the aboriginal tribe that lived on the mountain. There are two theories as to why it was renamed Guan Yin Mountain. According to the first theory, a candidate for Imperial Examination, Hu Zhuo-You, built a Taoist temple and named it Guan Yin Temple. Soon people began associating the whole mountain with Guan Yin. The second theory states that the rise and fall of the mountain ridge resembles the profile of an upwards-facing Guan Yin, especially when viewed from Guandu, and because of that likeness people began calling it Guan Yin Mountain.

The Legend of Guan Yin

Guan Shi Yin Buddha (Sanskrit: अवलोकतिश्वर ' Avalokiteśvara), another translation: Guan Zi Zai Buddha. Guan Yin is the most revered deity in East Asia and the head of the Five Deities in the Household. Guan Yin can be seen in household deity paintings together with household ancestors, and they are consecrated morning and night. Buddhist Scriptures talk of the mercy and immediate response of the holy Guan Yin in times of disaster. Guan Yin is the most venerated deity in Buddhism, and the reverence for it is clear in the widely-known saying, "Amitabha shields households and Guan Shi Yin harbors families."

Fu You Temple

Fu You Temple, built around 1732 and renovated in 1796, is the oldest of its kind in Tamsui. Its major deity is Mazu, the guardian goddess consecrated by immigrants and merchants who traveled by ship. The temple was the center of worship. The streets in front of the temple developed into the town of Tamsui. The front area of the temple was a port which became the beginnings of Tamsui. In the Sino-French War (1884-1885), it was said that the blessing of the temple protected the Chinese from invasion by the French Navy. Consequently the Guangxu Emperor issued a plaque of a board to the temple, on which was inscribed "Blessing from Above." Fu You Temple has been designated a Class III Heritage Site, and the boards, stone pillars, stone tablets and antiques add to the historic atmosphere. Among the items is an engraved tablet titled "Wang Gao Tower" which documents the planning and preparation to build a lighthouse.

Shisanhang Archeology Museum

Shisanhang Archeology Museum, located on the left bank of the Tamsui River estuary, is a Class II National Heritage Site. It was designated "Shisanhang Relic" after the investigation of Lin Chao-Qi, a geologist, in 1957. Historic antiques and burial items were unearthed one after another, illuminating much of the Iron Age of 500 to 1, 800 years ago. Its ethnic group might have connections with the Ketagalan tribe of the Pingpu tribes. Excavations found pottery, ironware, furniture, funerary objects, and the trading goods of foreign clans. Construction began in 1989 and the museum opened in April 2003. The areas around the museum were incorporated into the Pali Left Bank Culture and Ecology Park and features relics, a nature reserve, folk customs, industrial culture, and various public facilities.

Dialogue

Q Why is this area called Shisanhang?

A Shisanhang translates to thirteen foreign trading companies, and that refers to the fact that thirteen trading companies set up branch offices here at the end of the Qing Dynasty.

Q Were the early residents mariners?

A Sure they were. All the aborigines, 16 branches in total, were descendants of mariners. Using ocean currents, they took Banka (or canoes) on a very dangerous journey, sweeping over the seas from the coastal area of Mainland China to the islands nearby. The aborigines that lived here from 1, 500 to 2, 000 years ago were the ancestors of the Ketagalan tribe, one of the branches of the Pingpu tribes.

Q Is it possible to take a direct route to mainland China?

A Yes, since October 2013 there is a direct route to Pingtan, Fuzhou from Pali, Taipei. It only takes three hours. In the old days the route took quite a few days and involved traveling on sailboats.

Q Is Guan Shi Yin Buddha male or female?

A In Buddhism, Buddha and Bodhisattva are neutral in gender. While Guan Shi Yin was deemed male in the Tang dynasty (618-907), his appearance changes when he transforms into a feminine figure to offer advice to all living creatures. It may be that the nature of Guan Shi Yin's divine mercy symbolized maternal love, which explains why it was gradually transformed into a female figure.

Q Who was Mazu (the marine goddess)?

A Allegedly her name was Lin Mo-Niang, the daughter of a fishing family in Fukien during the Song Dynasty (960-1279). According to legend, she saved her father and brother while they were at sea by sacrificing her own life, and thus became associated with protecting and saving those on the water. The belief in Mazu expands all over Southern China and south-east Asia and includes over 200 million believers. In Taiwan alone there are over 900 Mazu temples.

Keywords

01. altitude [`æltə,tjud]: n. 海拔、高度

02. enshrine [ɪn`ʃraɪn]: v. 把……奉為神聖

03. deify [`diəfaɪ]: v. 將……奉若神明；deity [`diətɪ]: n. 神祇

04. silhouette [,sɪlʊ`ɛt]: n. 輪廓

05. descendant [dɪ`sɛndənt]: n. 後裔

06. ocean current [`kɜ·ənt]: n. 洋流

07. neutral [`njutrəl]: a. 中立的、中立地帶的、模糊的

08. gender [`dʒɛndə·]: n. 性別

09. alone [ə`lon]: a. / adv. 僅、單單

10. all living creatures: 世間眾生

11. scripture [`skrɪptʃə·]: n. 經典、經文、聖典

12. unveil [ʌn`vel]：v. 除去……的面紗、揭露出來

13. venerate [`vɛnə,ret]: n. 尊敬；崇敬

14. archeology [,ɑrkɪ`ɑlədʒɪ]：n. 考古學

15. entitle [ɪn`taɪt!]：v. 定名、給……稱號

16. unearth [ʌn`ɝθ] : v. 發掘

17. antique [æn`tik] : n. 文物

18. start: v. 草創、創辦

19. pottery [`pɑtərɪ]: n. 陶器

20. ironware [`aɪə-n͵wɛr] : n. 鐵器

21. furnace [`fɝnɪs]: n. 煉鐵爐、熔爐

22. funerary [`fjunə͵rɛrɪ] object: 墓葬品

23. reservation [͵rɛzə-`veʃən]: n. 自然保護區

24. diverse [daɪ`vɝs]: a. 多種多樣的、多變化的

25. folk [fok] custom [`kʌstəm]: n. 民俗

26. up to now: 迄今

27. excavate [`ɛkskə͵vet] : v. 出土、開鑿

28. merchant [`mɝtʃənt]: n. 商人

29. shroud [ʃraʊd]: v. 覆蓋、掩蔽

淡水河岸

THE TAMSUI RIVER BANK

The 1.5 kilometer river bank between Old Street and the small fishing port was named "The Golden Beach" by the Tamsui District Office because of its dazzling appearance at sunset. Along the beach is a wooded path, the river bank, a theatrical stage on the water, cafés, shops, and Tidal Art Square. 800-year-old banyans form a popular natural pavilion where people take shade and enjoy the sunset. The river bank is also beautified by the donation of three art sculptures by nearby shops: "The Fish" by Yu Lian-Chun, "The Boat and The Moon" by Uehara Kazuaki, and "Sunlight" by Lai Zhe-Xiang. The shops and scenery that line the path make a casual stroll along the bank a popular leisure activity.

The Reverie of Ye Jun-Lin

Ye Jun-Lin, a screenwriter, came to Tamsui with a cast and crew in 1957. He was enjoying a walk by the riverside when he came across a scene of astonishing beauty. As the sun was sinking below the sea and fishing boats were coming home for the day, he heard a faint song in the wind. Looking for the source of the beautiful voice, Ye caught a glimpse of a woman standing on a loft, waiting  behind a door. She was watching a cheerful and pleasant reunion at the ferry. Her expression inspired him to compose a song.

Tamsui in Paintings and Photography

Tamsui, a small township with magnificent scenery located at the intersection of a river and mountain, used to be Taiwan's top port, and is rich in history and arts. Its history as a booming sea port has brought diversity from all the east-west exchange and serves as inspiration for poems and photography. A mecca for professional painters and photographers, Tamsui has a profile similar to that of many European townships but with a style all its own. It invites artists with its American gothic church, vessels coming to anchor, ferries, the up and down ranges of Guan Yin Mountain, and the misty and foggy estuary. Tamsui, a place where any Western style painter would be happy to visit, remains unshakably true to itself.

The Folklore Music in Thriving

Folk music, which is defined by lyrics, melody and presentation done by fellow countrymen, has been popular in Taiwan for years. Initially the songs were passed from person to person and derived its energy from deep-rooted reflection. Folk songs have been in fashion since 1970 and have proven to be an important platform for native awareness and artistic creation. A key figure was Li Shuang-Ze (1949-1977), an alumnus of Tamkang University, who inspired his listeners and provoked thought by asking a philosophical question at a university concert. With a bottle of Coca-Cola in his hand, he asked, "Do we have any music of our own when we live in a time in which Taiwanese drink coke and listen to western music like westerners?" Then he sang his song Bu Po Wang (the Fishing Net) composed by Li Lin-Qiu (1909~1979).

The Sunset at Tamsui

Lyricist / Ye Jun-Lin   Melodist/ Hong Yi-Feng 1957

The sun is sinking in the west. The river water is dazzling with the sunlight.

Men and women, old and young, are waiting for the home-coming fishing crafts.

The windows and door are half shut on the loft.

Strings plucked are displaying a multitude of feelings and unknown bitterness.

The hazy, misty moonlight is above Shamao Mountain.

The river water is mirroring the gleaming moonlight. Nothing is as cool as the sea breeze.

A lone bird is taking a rest on the ferry.

The bird's song touches the heart softly.

The sunset at Tamsui glows with poetic touches.

The night fog falls. The church bell rings, transmitting into the seas.

Vague and faint are the lamplights on Buding, twinkling on and off like the stars blinking.

The memorable scene and sight arouse remorse and bitterness.

Dialogue

Q **There are a lot of tourists here. Do they come to Tamsui by MRT?**

A Yes, they do. The Tamsui Line was opened in 1997. At first business was bad due to a lack of popularity. These days it is often filled to capacity on weekends and holidays with passengers stacked like sardines.

Q **How many tourists is Tamsui able to accommodate?**

A On Chinese New Year of 2014, there was a record-breaking 100, 000 plus tourists on a single day. It was impossible to even take a step. It seemed as if Tamsui was submerged in a sea of people.

Q **Is it hard to be a tourist and do activities when it's that crowded?**

A It probably adds to the difficulty simply because there are too many people. But Tamsui is serene and carefree on weekdays and in the morning.

Q Tamsui is the birthplace of many folk songs and featured in many song lyrics. Are there any music schools in Tamsui?

A Only the Taipei National University of the Arts has a department of music. But this does not mean that music doesn't thrive in Tamsui. Tamsui is still the subject of much sentiment and inspires many people, especially in folk music. For example The Wanderers at Tamsui, composed by Chen Ming-Zhang, enjoyed wide-spread popularity in 1997.

Q How does the Tamsui River look now in comparison to the old days?

A I have the impression that in the old days, it was primarily a fishing port that had the unpleasant odor of fish. Today it is much cleaner and focused on tourists who appreciate both its natural beauty and a clean, modern environment.

Keywords

01. dazzling [`dæzlɪŋ]: a. 使人目眩的、令人眼花繚亂的

02. sculpture [`skʌlptʃɚ]: n. 雕塑品

03. artistic atmosphere [`ætməsˌfɪr]: n. 藝術氣息

04. exotic [ɛg`zɑtɪk]: a. 異國情調的、奇特的

05. stand in great numbers: 林立

06. stacked like sardine in a cage: 一位難求

07. accommodate [ə`kɑməˌdet]: v. 能容納、能提供……膳宿

08. not a trouble to it: 不礙事

09. genuine [`dʒɛnjʊɪn]: a. 真的、非偽造的、名副其實的

10. folk [fok] songs: n. 民歌

11. screenwriter [`skrinˌraɪtɚ]: n. 劇本作家、編劇家

12. expression [ɪk`sprɛʃən]: n. 表情、臉色

13. stir [stɝ]: v. 鼓動、煽動

14. create a unique style of its own: 自成一格

15. earnestly [`ɝnɪstlɪ]: adv. 認真地、誠摯地、熱心地

16. native [`netɪv] consciousness [`kɑnʃəsnɪs]: n. 本土意識

17. detonate [`dɛtə‚net]: v. 使爆炸、使觸發

18. reverberation [rɪ‚vɝbə`reʃən]: n. 共鳴、回響、餘韻

20. sustain [sə`sten] losses in business: 做生意賠錢

21. at present: 如今

22. on and off: 斷斷續續

23. loft [lɔft]: n. 閣樓、頂樓

24. Mecca [`mɛkə]: n. 朝聖地、發祥地

25. poetic [po`ɛtɪk]: a. 詩意的

26. rich in: 深厚

27. reflection [rɪ`flɛkʃən]: n. 深思、熟慮、反省

28. hazy [`hezɪ]: a. 有薄霧的、朦朧的

29. misty [`mɪstɪ]: a. 霧的、有霧的

30. be tangled with multitude of feelings: 百感交集

淡水老街

Tamsui
07

OLD STREET IN TAMSUI

Tamsui was demoted to a regional fishing port and lost much of its commercial function after Keelung Port opened. It has experienced a resurgence since being transformed into a tourist town. Old shops made of bricks can still be found sporadically in the Old Street area of Zhongzheng Road, now outnumbered by newer buildings. It is still possible to be transported back in time by walking the paths of Old Street, which is dotted with ancient temples. Intersecting Zongzheng Road, Chongjian street, Qingshui street and the MRT station, Old Street is a big attraction and conveniently accessible. Zongzheng Road is bustling with people, shops, and food. Antique stores and places selling hand-crafted goods have found their way into the district, creating an atmosphere of culture and nostalgia.

Chongjiang Street

Chongjiang Street is in the heart of the commercial district which was established long ago. Today visitors are able to walk it and savor the charm of Tamsui. It is a five to six hundred meter street that's full of history. As the "Street on the Top, " Chongjiang Street used to be the main route for surface transport. Going down will take you directly to the port and going up will take you to the village. The second half of the 19th century was a boom time for Tamsui and quite a few celebrities and important figures in politics, finance, and education made it their home. Located on an undulating hillside, a row of well-preserved old houses rise and fall in elevation.

"Full Praise for Chongjiang Street"

(Chinese Times/2013. Dec. 2/ by Xie Xing-En) Chongjiang Street, now over 230 years old, still harbors four historical sites. The New Taipei City Government, citing safety concerns, initiated the second phase of a road widening project which brought protestors that used the phrase, "Full Praise for Chongjiang Street." On the first day, hundreds of protestors voiced their desire to keep Chongjiang Street the way it was. It is a path that witnessed the history of Tamsui, flanked by ancient houses rich in custom and culture, including bullet holes left behind from the Sino-French War.

White House

The Tamsui White House, built by the slope on Sanming Street in 1875, got its name from its grayish-white exterior. It's believed that its construction was subsidized by Lin Ben-Yuan, a rich merchant in Panchiao, and that it was built by Yan Qing-Hua, one of Dr. MacKay's disciples. It was eventually leased to a Jewish trading company before being used as a storehouse. After catching on fire, it was taken apart and rebuilt. It is a popular subject for painters. In 2009 the Tamsui Culture Foundation commissioned a mural by painter Xiao Jin-Xing. It took several months to paint and now overlooks Tamsui as a vivid, breathtaking piece of public art.

Red House

Completed in 1899, Red House, which enjoys equal fame to White House, used to be the mansion of Li Yi-Han, a ship merchant. It was sold to Hong Yi-Nan, the counselor in the Office of Taipei, in 1913 after an accident in which two of Li's cargo ships crashed into each other and sank. Red House was renamed Da Guan Lou, a graceful name meaning resilient and philosophical. It was built with Western style similar to the exterior of the Tamsui British Consular Residence: spacious courtyard, interlinked stairways all around, and nice landscaping. After being owned by Hong Yi-Nan, it was then sold to Hong Bing-Jiang, famous for owning the De Yu Fish Ball Shop. In 1999 the building was reconditioned with advice from architects, historians, and artists. In 2000, Red House reopened as a fusion restaurant and art gallery.

Dialogue

Q Something is very interesting in the artistic-concerned figures who are working on preserving the Old Street. How did they gather together?

A There are workshops on literature and history in every city. They meet at these places or connect with one another through the Internet.

Q It's been said that Taiwan has one of the highest densities of Facebook users in the world, right?

A With the increasing number of people online and the popularity of instant messaging, those who used to talk loudly on the phone are now quietly fiddling on their smart phones.

Q The stairs on Chongjiang Street emit ancient and peculiar feelings. Its moderate incline makes it easy for people to climb it.

A Countless people have walked on those steps, which are one to two hundred years old. Their hustle and bustle penetrated every corner of Chongjiang Street. Indeed, the moderate incline makes it convenient for street vendors and senior tourists as well.

Q The slogan "Full Praise for Chongjiang Street" is a fantastic wordplay.

A Full Praise in Chinese implies presence and backup, which means that the slogan more or less means "Wholehearted Companionship with Chongjiang Street."

Q Red House has been renovated with attention paid to every detail, showing how magnificent and brilliant it was in its heyday.

A The terrific views from Red House make it an ideal place for watching the sunset and nightscape. Let me get you a cup of coffee.

Keywords

01. commercial function: n . 商務功能

02. silt [sɪlt] up: 泥沙淤積

03. regional [ˋridʒən!]: a. 地區的，局部的

04. decline [dɪˋklaɪn]: n. v. 沒落

05. new-fashioned: a. 新式

06. mirror [ˋmɪrɚ]: v. 反映

07. outdated: a. 舊式的、過時的

08. everyday life: n. 生活點滴

09. can be said to be: 堪稱

10. bustling and populous: a. 熱鬧

11. cuisine [kwɪˋzin]: n. 菜餚

12. snack [snæk]: n. 小吃

13. time-honored: a. 歷史悠久

14. zigzag [ˋzɪgzæg]: v. 蜿蜒

15. celebrity [sɪˋlɛbrətɪ]: n. 名人

16. nightscape: n. 夜景

17. density [ˋdɛnsətɪ]: n. 密度

18. fiddle [`fɪd!] on the smart phones: 滑手機

19. spontaneously [spɒn`teniəslɪ]: adv. 自發地；不由自主地

20. moderate [`mɑdərɪt]: a. 溫和

21. safety concern: 安全疑慮

22. road broadening: 道路拓寬

23. rise and decline: 興衰

24. trigger [`trɪgɚ]: v. 扣扳機開（槍）、觸發、引起

25. commission [kə`mɪʃən]: v. 委任，委託

26. vivid-like: a. 生動

27. breath-taking: a. 震憾人心

28. fusion restaurant: n. 複合式餐廳

29. interlinked: a. 相通

30. courtyard [`kort`jɑrd]: n. 庭院

31. spacious [`speʃəs]: a. 寬敞的

32. accessible [æk`sɛsəb!]: a. 可（或易）得到的、
可（或易）使用的

Tamsui
08

殼牌倉庫

THE SHELL WAREHOUSE

The Shell Warehouse is located in Bi Zai Tou next to the Tamsui MRT, and takes up around 3, 000 pings. The building was first leased by the British Cass Trading Company in 1894 for exporting tea. In 1897 it was bought by Shell, which built four large oil tanks for their kerosene business and installed railways linked to the Tamsui railway. Exuding an unpleasant odor, the Shell Warehouse had an interesting nickname: "the smelly oil warehouse." After being bombarded by US forces during an air raid in October 1944 (World War II), it took three days to extinguish the fire in the oil tanks. In 2000 the warehouse was designated a historical site and donated to the Tamsui Culture Foundation by the Shell Oil Company. In 2001 it became the Tamsui Community University, and in 2011 that became part of the Tamsui Culture Park.

Tamsui Community University

Tamsui Community University opened in August of 2001. Its comprehensive curriculum, uniqueness, and low cost all make it a great institution of public education. Its stated goals are to promote lifelong learning, culture, community development, and education. The campus is characterized by a mix of historical sites, native culture, and Tamsui-oriented courses. It is an institution that is tremendously proud of its heritage.

Tamsui Culture Park

The Tamsui Culture Park (which contains the Shell Warehouse and the nearby greens and wetland) was formed and opened in 2011. It takes up around 1.8 hectares, and includes eight historic buildings and the remains of the railways used for oil and lubricants distribution. The buildings have been renovated and consist of six oil warehouses, a pump room, and a boiler room. The Tamsui Shell

Warehouse has seen hard times, war, and changes in ownership, but now it's ready to shine as an educational institute (Tamsui Community University), exhibition hall, stage, art gallery, and nature reserve.

Yinshan Temple
The Hakka Assembly Hall

Yinshang Temple, built in 1822 and designated a Class II Heritage Site, consecrates Dingguang Buddha, the major deity of the Hakka people of South China. The temple looks much as it did in the days of Emperor Daoguang, including the clay sculptures on the ridge of the roof. It is the only assembly hall from the Qing Dynasty that is fully preserved. An assembly hall is like a club where townspeople could gather and voice their concerns. This hall was built with safety in mind. Due to the large numbers of Hakka immigrants from Tingzhou going to the north of Taiwan during Emperor Daoguang's reign, there was a need to avoid problems and bullying that occured when they came in contact with immigrants from Zhangzhou and Quanzhou. First the village, then the assembly hall were built for that purpose. It also became a temporary stopover for immigrants from Tangshan.

Dialogue

Q **It is a terrific idea to combine historical sites with ecology.**

A Yes, it is. With this in mind, the government approved the Bi Zai Tou Historical Site and Ecology Park, which incorporates five historical sites: Yinshan Temple, the Hunan Yong Tombs, the Tamsui Shell Warehouse, the Tamsui Amphibious Airport, and the Tamsui Meteorological Observatory.

Q **The Taiwanese are concerned with environmental protection and nature activities, aren't they?**

A They have become more environmentally aware in the past 10 years, as evidenced by the creation of the Environmental Protection Administration and the works of the Ministry of Culture. Nature and ecology are definitely things that they think about.

Q **Tamsui is becoming a part of the global village!**

A Tamsui has always been internationally minded. Modern Taiwan is an open democracy. But a side effect of being a part of the modern world is that it can be easy to lose touch with history, something that requires a lot of work to preserve.

Q **Isn't it true that the majority of students at Tamsui Community University are senior citizens?**

A It is. On one hand, quality of life, physical health and early retirement motivates government employees to take part in social activities. On the other hand, increased life expectancy also increases the needs of senior citizens. There is a motto popular in Chinese society: "Life is short. Art is long."

Q **I see. Besides being a wonderful place for the young, Tamsui will also be a great place for them when they become senior citizens.**

A Frankly speaking, the serenity of Tamsui is often disturbed by noise, especially the noise of traffic. But to redirect traffic would sacrifice some of the environment.

Keywords

01. kerosene [ˋkɛrəˌsin]: n. 煤油
02. unpleasant [ʌnˋplɛznt] odor [ˋodɚ]: n. 惹人厭的惡臭
03. extinguish [ɪkˋstɪŋgwɪʃ]: v. 撲滅（火等）
04. take up: v. 佔（地方）、費（時間）
05. permeate [ˋpɝmɪˌet]: v. 浸透、充滿、彌漫
06. bombard [bɑmˋbɑrd]: v. 砲擊、轟炸
07. life expectancy [ɪkˋspɛktənsɪ]: n. 平均壽命
08. motivate [ˋmotəˌvet]: v. 給……動機、刺激、激發
09. Life is short. Art is long.: 活到老，學到老
10. touch [tʌtʃ]: n. 風格、特點
11. fade away: 褪去（顏色）
12. democratize [dɪˋmɑkrəˌtaɪz]: v. 使民主化
13. Ministry of Culture: 文化部
14. Environmental Protection Administration: 環保署
15. terrific [təˋrɪfɪk]: a. 非常好的、了不起的
16. metrological [ˌmɛtrəˋlɑdʒɪk!]: a. 度量衡學的

17. observatory [əb`zɝvə͵torɪ]: n. 氣象臺、觀測所

18. approve [ə`pruv]: v. 批准；認可

19. pump room: n. 幫浦間

20. boiler room: n. 鍋爐間

21. devastate [`dɛvəs͵tet]: v. 破壞、蹂躪

22. intact [ɪn`tækt]: a. 完整無缺的、原封不動的

23. show the mutual concern to each other: 互相濟助

24. stop over: v. 臨時落腳

25. comprehensive [͵kɑmprɪ`hɛnsɪv]: a. 廣泛的、無所不包的、綜合的

26. administrative [əd`mɪnə͵stretɪv] affair: n. 行政事務

27. regulation [͵rɛgjə`leʃən]: n. 規章、規則、規定、條例

28. unceasingly [ʌn`sisɪŋlɪ]: adv. 繼續地、不斷地

29. curricular [kə`rɪkjələ]: a. 課程的

30. realize [`rɪə͵laɪz]: v. 落實、實現

Tamsui
09

滬尾砲台

HOBE FORTRESS

Hobe Fortress, located in the north of Tamsui, was built in 1886 on eight hectacres by Lui Ming-Chuan, the first inspector-general of Taiwan. It was built to defend Tamsui Port. Despite not being used in years, it is a well-preserved stronghold. Lui left an inscription on a tablet above the garrison gate: Bei Men Suo Yao (Gateway to Northern Taiwan). The Spanish were the first to build a cannon fortress on the site, and it was used by the Dutch until they burned it down when they withdrew from Taiwan. The Qing Dynasty fortified it for garrison duty in 1808, followed by construction of another cannon fortress. After the Sino-French War, Lui was tasked with coastal defense. When it came under Japanese rule, the four cannons of Hobe Fortress were removed and it was used as an artillery training field. When the Kuomintang took over, the fortress was again used for national defense. It was finally designated a Class II Heritage site in 1985, restored, and opened to the public.

Youchekou

Youchekou, a place in Tamsui that saw much warfare, was developed by immigrants from Quanzhou and named after an oil mill run by Guo, also a Quanzhou immigrant. The Youchekou port is a popular spot for wedding photos because it is where Guan Yin Mountain, the Tamsui River, fishing boats, and a beautiful sunset can be captured. Zhongyi Temple, which enshrines Su Fu Wang Ye, is the largest temple of its kind in Tamsui. It conducts specific religious ceremonies on the Double Ninth Festival on 9th September according to the Chinese lunar calendar. Around 30 years ago, there was an old black house in the area that sold snacks of excellent quality at a reasonable price. It was named Dark Palace and renowned for pork chops. It later moved to a nearby spot. At meal time Dark Palace is often swarmed with customers.

Sino-French War

In an attempt to occupy northern Taiwan, French battle ships struck Tamsui as part of the Sino-French War. Concerned about the gateway to northern Taiwan, inspector-general Lui Ming-Chuan decided to stop defending Keelung and deployed his forces to Tamsui. After the fortresses in Shalun, Zhonglun and Youchekou were battered down, Lui commissioned Sun Kai-Hua, the local commander in charge of the defense of Tamsui, to block the Port with naval mines and construct fortifications along the shore. On 8th October, Sun and some Qing regular forces and militiamen repelled the French forces. This was a precious military victory. Sanctions of the coastal area were lifted after the French withdrawal six months later.

Bei Men Suo Yao
(The Gateway to Northern Taiwan)

The Chinese characters used in the phrase "The gateway to northern Taiwan" implies that there is a stronghold defending northern Taiwan. In 1885 after the Sino-French War, the Qing Dynasty started fortifying their defenses. Lui Ming-Chung commissioned engineer Max E. Hecht (1853-1892) to supervise the construction. Thirty-five cannons were imported from the UK and assembled on site in 1889. The foundation and structures never saw battle again, so they are nicely preserved. Bei Men Suo Yao, the inscription on the tablet atop the south-east barracks gate, is in Lui's own handwriting. The survival of this inscription is rare among the fortresses built by Lui in Taiwan, all of which were important. Max E. Hecht is buried in Tamsui's Foreigners' Cemetery and was given a reward and medal of honor for his contributions to Taiwan's defense.

Dialogue

Q **Occupying a commanding vantage point, this is the perfect place for a fortress.**

A Here is Wujiu Mound, the first mound of Five-Tiger Hill. The Tamsui Golf Course, the first of its kind in Taiwan, was built by the Japanese in 1919 on what used to be a training field for the Qing Dynasty.

Q **Many Tamsui residents have connections to Hunan, right?**

A Most of the regular army deployed from Mainland China to Taiwan were from Hunan. Sun Kai-Hua, the general charged with guarding Tamsui in the Sino-French War in 1884, was from Hunan. There is an ancient tomb of Hunan warriors in the graveyard at Ganzhenlin.

Q **Taiwanese are well known for their wedding photos aren't they? So much so that they even get a lot of business from Mainland China?**

A The wedding photo industry is a big business. There is even a street full of wedding photo studios. Most of the industry was developed by Taiwanese.

Q **Is it necessary to go out and find wonderful scenery for wedding photos?**

A There are outdoor scenes that must be shot on location. Of course you want to find the nicest scenery possible. Couples with enough financial resources are able to do photo shoots in the same foreign countries that they have their honeymoon. As a result, many photographers are qualified tour guides.

Q **Can wedding photos play a role in maintaining a successful marriage?**

A Taiwan used to have a pretty low divorce rate, but it has gone up in recent times. It makes sense that browsing their old wedding album may make a bickering couple think twice about divorce.

Keywords

01. preserve [prɪ`zɝv]: v. 保留
02. garrison [`gærɪsn] duty: n. 駐防
03. coastal defense [dɪ`fɛns]: n. 海防
04. national defense: n. 國防任務
05. entrust [ɪn`trʌst]: v. 賦予
06. even-shifting: a. 舉足輕重
07. occupy a commanding vantage position: 居高臨下
08. drill [drɪl] ground: n. 練兵場
09. regular army: n. 正規軍
10. wedding photo: n. 婚紗照
11. export [ɪks`port]: v. 輸出、外銷
12. prosperous [`prɑspərəs]: a. 興旺的、繁榮的

13. divorce [də`vors] rate: n. 離婚率

14. browse [braʊz] over: v. 隨便翻翻

15. commission [kə`mɪʃən]: v. 任命、委任、委託

16. defense work: n. 防禦工事

17. militiaman [mɪ`lɪʃəmən]: n. 鄉勇、民兵

18. repel [rɪ`pɛl]: v. 擊退、驅除

19. assemble [ə`sɛmb!]: v. 安裝

20. supervise [`supəˌvaɪz]: v. 監造、監督

21. battle field: n. 戰場

22. excellent quality and reasonable price: 物美價廉

23. bicker [`bɪkə]: v. 吵嘴、爭吵

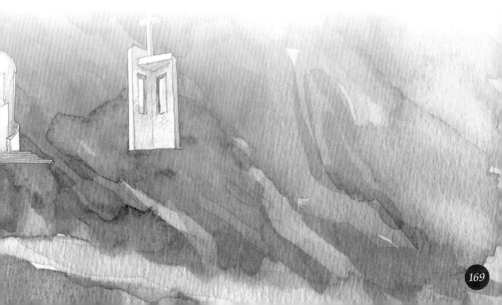

Tamsui
10

漁人碼頭

FISHERMAN'S WHARF

Tamsui Fisherman's Wharf, located on the east bank of the Tamsui River estuary near the Shalun bathing beach and a second fishing port developed in 1987, is a newly developed tourist attraction renowned for its splendid sunset and fresh seafood. Besides the tourist and leisure facilities, it still functions as an active fishing port. Its floating pier is able to accommodate 150 fishing boats and cruise ships, and the riverside platform can hold an audience of 3, 000. The white cable-stayed bridge opened on February 14th 2003, Valentine's Day, and is called Lover's Bridge. The 164.9m long bridge is an ideal place for enjoying the sunset. Nearby there is a five-star hotel. Both the land route and waterways lead to Fisherman's Wharf, one of the reasons that it enjoys high popularity.

Lovers' Bridge

Lovers' Bridge is 164.9 meters in length, five meters in width and 12 meters at its highest point. It is a bridge built exclusively for pedestrians, and for many it is the most recognizable part of Fisherman's Wharf. Its slightly curved pillars feel like a streamlined sail. Its light purple and pink hue looks like white in the distance. Its graceful, romantic profile and great views make it one of Tamsui's star attractions. It is said that any lovers who cross the bridge hand-in-hand will have a glorious future.

Lovers' Tower

The Lover's Tower at Fisherman's Wharf was opened in May 2011, cost over 300 million NT dollars, is 100 meters in height, and has a capacity of 80 people. Made by the Swiss over a period of four years, it offers a one-of-a-kind rotating platform with an encased, circular chamber to keep out the wind and rain. Its height and rotation allows guests a 360 degree view of their surroundings.

The Leisure Fishing Port

Even though it retains the function of a fishing port, Fishermen's Wharf has been transformed into a cruise liner pier. Its floating pier accommodates all sorts of yachts whose owners are the rich and powerful who love the sea. The pier is like a parking lot for their yachts. In their free time, they enjoy cruising the waters. It is an important scenic spot on the Blue Highway and a popular stopover as well. The sapphire blue sky during the day, emerald green wa-

ter, fishing boats and yachts, and crimson red sky in the evening all compose a rare, marvelous coastal view of northern Taiwan.

The Tamkang Bridge

The Tamkang Bridge, which has yet to be constructed, will be a double-deck bridge passing over the estuary of the Tamsui River, the first of its kind that involves both a railway and a highway. Proposed at the end of the 1980s with construction to begin in 2016 and finishing in 2020, the Tamkang Bridge will be 44 meters wide, 20 meters high, and allow highway speeds of 100 kilometers per hour on the lower deck and a light rail system eight meters in width on the upper deck. This 15 billion and 300 million NT dollar expenditure is designed to ease traffic congestion and spark the development of Tamhai New Town.

Dialogue

Q Tamsui's charm and charisma is evident when you look at it from above. The whole town looks calm, pleasant, and blissful.

A The Taiwan in Beyond Beauty, a documentary made from a bird's eye view, is novel and impressive. Taiwan remains as magnificent as it was 400 years ago when Portuguese mariners sailed by, exclaiming "Isla Formosa" with admiration, meaning "what a beautiful island."

Q Yes! The documentary also preaches moderation and warns against over-development.

A It does. Moderate and well-planned development is a must. The construction of Tamkang Bridge was finally approved only after 20 years of negotiation.

Q The bridge should be a top priority. Tamsui will be come even more prosperous after its completion.

A We hope that everything will go as planned and that development will be thoughtfully restrained. The negative side effects of overpopulation can be seen in human history.

Q Isn't Tamsui overwhelmingly crowded in the summer and cold and cheerless in the winter?

A Yes, it is as popular as many of the renowned resorts of foreign countries in the summer and autumn, featuring music concerts, art markets and of course the famous sunset. But it is quite lonely and deserted in the rainy spring and chilly winter. However, the local tourist industry has come up with policies and measures to address this imbalance.

Q Isn't it said that Tamsui has authentic seafood?

A Tamsui is in essence a fishing port whose seafood is undoubtedly fresh. It's up to you to give it a try!

Keywords

01. cable-stayed bridge: n. 斜張橋
02. cruise ship: n. 遊艇
03. accommodate [əˋkɑməˌdet]: v. 能容納
04. floating piers [pɪr]: n. 浮動碼頭
05. retain [rɪˋten]: v. 保有
06. facility [fəˋsɪlətɪ]: n. 設施
07. bathing beach: n. 海水浴場
08. newly-developed: a. 最新開發
09. bird's eye view: n. 俯視、鳥瞰
10. over-exploitation [ˌɛksplɔɪˋteʃən]: n. 過度開發
11. prove [pruv]: v. 證明、證實
12. alert [əˋlɝt]: n. 警戒、警報；a. 警覺的、警惕的
13. coordinated measures: n. 配套措施
14. chilly [ˋtʃɪlɪ]: a. 冷颼颼的、冷得使人不舒服的
15. fervently [ˋfɝvəntlɪ]: adv. 熱烈地、熱情地
16. sapphire [ˋsæfaɪr] blue sky: n. 藍天 (sapphire 藍寶石)
17. emerald [ˋɛmərəld] green marine: n. 碧海 (emerald 綠寶石)
18. crimson [ˋkrɪmzn] red sky: n. 滿天湛紅 (crimson 緋紅色)
19. overpass [ˌovɚˋpæs]: v. 跨越

20. expenditure [ɪk`spɛndɪtʃə]: n. 支出額、經費

21. interchange [ˌɪntə`tʃendʒ]: n. 聯絡道、（高速公路上的）交流道

22. streamlined [`strim‚laɪnd]: a. 流線的

23. hue [hju]: n. 色調

24. graceful [`gresfəl]: a. 優美

25. expansive [ɪk`spænsɪv]: a. 遼闊 (expensive: a. 昂貴的)

26. lovely [`lʌvlɪ]: a. 美麗

27. landmark [`lænd‚mɑrk]: n. 地標

28. promising [`prɑmɪsɪŋ]: a. 有前途的、大有可為的

29. glamorous [`glæmərəs]: a. 富有魅力的；迷人的

30. safety glass: n. 安全玻璃

31. protection casing: n. 防護罩

32. take in the whole scene at once: 盡收眼底

33. chamber [`tʃembə]: n. 座艙

34. exclusive [ɪk`sklusɪv] for pedestrians [pə`dɛstrɪən]: 專供行人步行 (exclusive 專用的)

35. active [`æktɪv]: a. 現役的

紅樹林

Tamsui
11

HONGSHULIN OR THE MANGROVE

The bright, green, lush mangrove catches the eye of every tourist as the MRT trains enter Hongshulin Station. It was designated the Tamsui River Mangrove Conservation Area and covers an area of 76 hectares of sandbanks and swamp formed by silt deposited in the river. It is the biggest of its kind in Taiwan and represents the northern most line of naturally occurring mangrove in the world. This vigorously growing aquatic plant gets its name, "the red woods" (the literal Chinese translation), due to its red branches. The mangrove wetland ecosystem is very useful to humans. It protects embankments, supplies fish and habitat for wildlife, wood for fuel, and provides a good place for people to "get back to nature." It also has several other Chinese nicknames which translate to "paradise for migratory birds" and "water forest."

The Egrets

Egrets, common birds in Taiwan, usually live in groups around wetlands and lakes, feeding on fish, batrachians and insects. The Tamsui mangrove is a major home to egrets; their numbers are estimated to be in the hundreds. When they fly home in small groups in the evening, their intermittent cries break the serenity of the sky. Their spotless white feathers imply purity, elegance, agility and gracefulness. It is said that egrets only live in places that are blessed. Where there are rice paddies there are egrets hovering for insects, a fine form of pest control.

Kandelia Obovata or Pen Seedlings

The woods that lay on the riverbank between Zhuwei and Tamsui are composed of pen seedlings, which get their amusing name from their 10 to 15cm seedlings that have a pen-like profile and hang from branches. The viviparous seedlings sprout from the maternal plants and are able to absorb nutrition from them while hanging. The seedlings stick into the mud when they break away and grow lateral roots, eventually turning into trees. Those that don't get stuck in the mud are carried by currents and end up taking root wherever they land. The viviparity is most advantageous in high salinity, soft soil, high chlorine, oxygen-depleted water.

The Ecology Pathway

The Tamsui Hongshulin Ecology Pathway, a hardwood path whose entrance is by the Hongshulin MRT Station, zig-zags inside Hongshulin Eco Park. At its shortest it is one kilometer long, and views of Guan Yin Mountain, the riverside, and bio-diverse wetlands can all be found along the way. It is possible to closely observe and touch pen seedlings next to the path. There is a lively dynamic that occurs as fiddler crabs scurry about and egrets can be seen keeping a close watch on their prey. It is a favorite place for bird watchers and wetland field trips. The ideal period for bird watching is between September and the following May, when migratory birds pass through the area.

Dialogue

Q Egrets are a favorite of the Taiwanese, aren't they?
The highways of Tamsui are decorated with wall
paintings featuring egrets in flight.

A They are. There is a well-known Taiwanese nursery rhyme:
"An egret was trying to land in a river but stumbled. After
crashing, it found a penny." The lyrics mean that children who
have nothing to play with would like to transform into egrets
and encounter good luck.

Q Is the Tamsui mangrove a stopover for migratory
birds?

A A survey by the Wild Bird Federation states that there are
around 10 species that do so, but not in great numbers due
to its proximity to the city, the dense population, and difficulties
in hunting for food. However, small birds are common,
especially in the Guandu plain where quite a few cottages were
built for close observation.

Q **The Guandu plain is classified as a wetland and must be protected, right?**

A Yes, it is. It was listed as one of the least-developed areas by the government. With the increased care of wetlands, much has been done to protect and put them to good use. For instance they are a good place to teach conservation and for family activities.

Q **Wasn't the Guandu plain a great swamp and Qilian a port?**

A As a matter of fact the Taipei basin used to be dotted with swamps, and quite a few areas are lower than sea level, making it prone to floods. The Taipei Metro has been flooded before, causing traffic problems for weeks.

Q **Taipei was totally flooded, wasn't it?**

A Flood control policy is very important in Taiwan, but we are still very fond of water activities.

Keywords

01. mark out: v. 劃為
02. sandbank [`sænd,bæŋk]: n. 沙洲、沙丘
03. aquatic [ə`kwætɪk] plant: n. 水生植物
04. fish fry [fraɪ]: n. 魚苗
05. habitat [`hæbə,tæt]: n. 棲息地（動物的）、產地（植物的）
06. egret [`igrɛt]: n. 白鷺鷥
07. nursery rhyme [raɪm]: n. 童謠
08. cottage [`kɑtɪdʒ]: n. 小屋
09. put sth to good account: 積極地加以利用
10. stagnation [stæg`neʃən]: n. 淤塞；
    停滯 (stagnant a. 不流動的，停滯的)
11. flood containment [kən`tenmənt]: n. 治水
    (contain v. 控制、遏制)
12. resident bird: n. 留鳥
13. batrachian [bə`trekɪən]: n. 蛙類

14. rice paddy [`pædɪ]: n. 稻田、水田

15. agile [`ædʒaɪl]: a. 敏捷

16. staid [sted]: a. 穩重

17. spotlessly white: a. 潔白

18. seedling [`sidlɪŋ]: n. 幼苗

19. viviparous [vaɪ`vɪpərəs]: a. 胎生

20. maternal [mə`tɝn!] plant: n. 母株　(maternal a. 母親的)

21. nutrition [nju`trɪʃən]: n. 養份

22. break away: v. 脫離

23. salinity [sə`lɪnətɪ]: n. 鹽度

24. hardwood [`hɑrd͵wʊd]: n. 實木

25. fiddler [`fɪdlɚ] crab: n. 招潮蟹
    (fiddler n. 小提琴手。招潮蟹的大螯狀似小提琴。)

26. tidal [`taɪd!] flat: n. 潮間帶

27. pass through: 過境

185

Tamsui
12

淡水小吃

THE SNACKS IN TAMSUI

With its history as a fishing port, Tamsui is blessed with many resources both local and foreign. It is renowned for fresh seafood and a rich culture of food and drink. The influence of foreigners and locals have created various styles of gastronomic culture. Among a plethora of renowned snacks are fish balls, crispy fish, iron eggs, and a-ge. Iron eggs and a-ge are tastes that are found exclusively on Old Street. Most foods are obtained locally and reflect the daily needs of ordinary people. Cultural integration and social inclusion can be seen in the diet, and quality can be found in everything from ordinary meals to exotic seafood banquets.

The Fish Balls

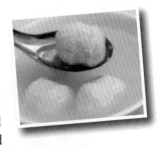

In Tamsui's days as a fishing port the fish harvest was so successful that supply often exceeded demand. This means that besides being sold at market, all parts of the fish were used to make various snacks, such as dried fish and crisp fish. Big fish such as shark or dolphin fish were often made into surimi, blended with corn starch and water, and made into fish balls. Some fish balls are stewed with ground pork, but they taste great when cooked in any kind of broth. Today fish balls are made with all kinds of ingredients, and can be found all over the world.

Iron Egg

An apo (old lady) used to sell noodles on the side of the road next to the ferry, and any eggs left over would get stewed again and again until they were reduced to small black orbs that looked hard as iron. Out of curiosity, customers bought some to try and found them to be chewy and full of flavor. Soon these "iron eggs" became known far and wide. This snack, another dish unique to Tamsui, was named after the old lady: "Apo Iron Egg." The process of making these eggs is quite involved. They must be stewed in a special recipe of spices, and then dried in the wind. The whole thing takes several days.

Traditional Cakes

There are numerous traditional cake shops with long-established reputations in Tamsui. The cakes are made in many different flavors and the techniques used to make them have been refined from ancient methods. Each bite is full of nostalgia and local flavor, and they are an important part of Tamsui's food culture. In 1984 Xin Sheng Fa, one of Tamsui's renowned shops, even won the golden medal in the Japanese Cake Olympics. In Taiwanese wedding custom Tamsui cakes must be ordered and given to in-laws and close friends.

The Fish Ball Museum

Dengfeng, a fishery company, developedcrisp fish in 1963 as an accompaniment to staple foods. It later be-came a popular snack in its own right and was often given as gifts. The Fish Ball Museum was founded by Dengfeng in 2004, and it is the first of its kind. There is a fish ball DIY activity in the tourist's workshop. The museum, which takes up about 70 pings, has three stories: the first is a shop, the second an exhi-

bition hall showcasing fishery instruments, and the third has containers, illustrated photos and a standard rifle（Fusil Gras M80 1874） left by French marines after the Sino-French War (1884).

A-ge

A-ge is the simplified translation of the Japanese word for fried bean curd (or oily tofu). It is made by hollowing out a tofu, stuffing it with bean noodles, and sealing it with surimi. It is then steamed, seasoned with a sweet and spicy sauce, and show-ered with fish ball or bone broth. A-ge is unique to Tamsui. It was invented by Yang Zheng Jin-Wen in 1965 while trying to figure out what to do with some leftovers. The founding shop is located on Zhenli Street, still doing business with students looking for breakfast or lunch.

Dialogue

Q **A lot of tourists come for the snacks, don't they?**

A Taiwanese cuisine ranks first or second in the world, with only Mediterranean and Japanese cuisine as rivals. The diversity of the Taiwanese diet can't be found in Mainland China or Hong Kong.

Q **What distinguishes snacks from meals?**

A Meals are served in a banquet and can involve 10 to 12 courses, while snacks are generally a single item and can be described as "street food, " especially in night markets where many different kinds of snacks can be found.

Q **Taiwanese snacks are even recommended to foreign guests of honor at state banquets, aren't they?**

A They are a genuine part of Taiwanese cuisine that can't be found anywhere else.

Q How many different kinds of Taiwanese snacks are there? Where can we find them?

A No comprehensive survey has been done. Even some seemingly identical snacks can have different tastes and ingredients. The night markets are where they are mostly found. Some restaurants have started selling Taiwanese snacks, but not all of them are good.

Q So the night markets are on the must-see list.

A I have to warn you that sometimes hygiene and quality of service can be a problem at the night market. Be prepared!

Keywords

01. nurture [`nɝtʃɚ]: v. 孕育
02. profound history: n. 歷史悠久
03. proletariat [ˌprolə`tɛrɪət]: n. 普羅大眾
04. various [`vɛrɪəs]: a. 多樣
05. rival [`raɪvl]: v. 媲美、與……匹敵、比得上
06. distinguish [dɪ`stɪŋgwɪʃ]: v. 使傑出、使顯出特色
07. diverse [daɪ`vɝs]: a. 多種多樣的、多變化的
08. recommend [ˌrɛkə`mɛnd]: v. 推薦、介紹
09. dignitary [`dɪgnəˌtɛrɪ]: n. 顯貴、要人
10. state banquet [`bæŋkwɪt]: n. 國宴
11. identical [aɪ`dɛntɪkl]: a. 完全相同的、完全相似的
12. presentable [prɪ`zɛntəbl]: a. 搬得上檯面的
13. fall behind one's expectation: 期望落空
14. fishery harvesting: n. 漁獲
15. exhibition hall: n. 展示廳
16. standard rifle: n. 制式步槍
17. surimi [`srɪmɪ]: n. 魚漿

18. broth [brɔθ]: n. 湯汁

19. appetizing [ˋæpəˌtaɪzɪŋ]: a. 食指大動

20. handiwork [ˋhændɪˌwɝk]: n. 手工

21. ingredient [ɪnˋgridɪənt]: n. 配料

22. roadside food stand: n. 路邊攤

23. reduce [rɪˋdjus]: v. 減少；縮小；降低

24. chewy [ˋtʃuɪ]: a. 耐嚼的

25. wind-dried: a. 風乾的

26. spiced recipe [ˋrɛsəpɪ]: n. 五香配方

27. aromatic [ˌærəˋmætɪk]: a. 芳香的；馨香的

28. an old shop with long-established reputation: n. 老字號

29. refine [rɪˋfaɪn]: v. 提煉，精鍊；精製

30. nostalgia [nɑsˋtældʒɪə]: n. 懷舊之情

31. cuisine [kwɪˋzin]: n. 美食

32. etiquette [ˋɛtɪkɛt]: n. 禮節、禮節、禮儀

33. gastronomic [ˌgæstrəˋnɑmɪk]: a. 烹飪學的

34. plethora [ˋplɛθərə]: n. 過多

Tamsui
13

淡水藝文

THE ARTS AT TAMSUI

In ancient times Tamsui was both the northern gateway for Han immigrants and an important stronghold of power. When it came under Japanese rule for half a century its importance declined. But its days as a trading port made it rich in culture, historical sites, and relics. Its terrain, landscape, and history have always made it a favorite place for artists, writers, performers, and musicians. Modern events and activities such as the Tamsui Arts Carnival, Asia Art Village and Cloud Gate Dance Theater ensure that its legacy of being an important place for the arts will continue.

Tamsui Itteki Memorial House

The Tamsui Itteki Memorial House, located on the left side of the Hobe Fortress, is a century-old building from Fukui, Japan. The former residence of Japanese writer Mizukami Tsutomu, its unique name, Itteki (meaning a drop of water), comes from this quote by Mizukami Tsutomu: "A tiny drop of water harbors a huge momentum." The memorial house, which survived the 1995 Great Hanshin earthquake in Japan, was donated to Taiwan for spiritual support after the 921 earthquake hit Taiwan in 1999. The Tamsui Itteki Memorial House was fully reassembled on August 16th 2009 and opened to the public on March 29th 2011.

Volunteers from Hanshin also helped a lot in the rebuilding. 1, 300 Taiwanese and Japanese volunteers worked together to help the area recover.

The Tamsui Temple Parade

Temple parades are meant to honor the gods, and part of tradition involves sanctifying them with open-air banquets. This inevitably leads to extravagant meals and large gatherings of friends and family. The tradition first started long ago when people sought to ward off disease, disaster, and warfare by appealing to their hometown guardian deities. Nowadays the temple parades have become an integral part of life despite the religious aspect fading into the

background. The Tamsui Parade starts with a ceremony at Qing Shui Zu Shi Temple on May 6th of the lunar calendar (the middle of June on the solar calendar), and everyone in town shows up for it, making intensive traffic control necessary.

The Tamsui Art Festival

The Tamsui Art Parade and Carnival is a festival that began in 2008 and comes back every October. In 2013 its theme was "World Kaleidoscope, " and 1, 500 people in 50 teams celebrated diversity and culture with creativity and enthusiasm. The art carnival is possible because of the united efforts of numerous artists and residents who embody the history, legends, customs, and everyday lives of Tamsui. An artistic banquet which incorporates international art groups is represented in the art parade

and historical drama, which tells the story of a 400-year history.

Dialogue

Q **The unique and close connection between Taiwan and Japan is revealed in the touching story of the It-teki Memorial House.**

A Taiwan and Japan have always been closely connected and they both enjoy the benefits of tourism, business, and mutual understanding.

Q **Cloud Gate Dance Theater, the world-renowned art group, will boost artistic activity and bring more exposure to Tamsui with its Tamsui branch.**

A Apparently it was Cloud Gate that chose to come to Tamsui. The Cloud Gate Tamsui branch will soon be opened to the public for visits and workshops.

Q **Why do Taiwanese people consecrate their deities by sacrificing pigs, while Westerners and other peoples do it with cows or lambs?**

A Pigs used to be common livestock among the Taiwanese, so they were an appropriate representation of family. No family would be blessed without a pig. With cows and lambs being relatively scarce and favored in farming, pigs did the work.

Q It is said that the rearing of heavy pigs for competition is something that people from all walks of life do, isn't it?

A They do it as an honor and tribute to their deity. The heaviest pig in history weighed 1, 683 Taiwanese kilograms (equal to 1, 010 kilograms), and required a great amount of careful preparation. The meat is usually given away to in-laws and close friends at open air banquets.

Q Will it be a good idea if the worshiping is involved with artistic carnival?

A It surely will. You are a potential Minister of Culture.

Keywords

01. decline [dɪ`klaɪn]: v. 淪落
02. colony [`kɑlənɪ]: n. 殖民地
03. powers [`paʊɚs]: n. 列強
04. vigorous[`vɪgərəs] vitality [vaɪ`tæ.lətɪ]: n. 旺盛的生命力
05. international perspective [pɚ`spɛktɪv]: n. 國際觀
06. mutual [`mjutʃʊəl]: a. 相互的、彼此的
07. initiate [ɪ`nɪʃɪɪt]: v. 開始著手（某一計畫）
08. sanctify [`sæŋktə.faɪ]: v. 使神聖化
09. worship [`wɝʃɪp]: v. 敬仰、禮拜
10. carnival [`kɑrnəv!]: n. 嘉年華會
11. blaze [blez] one's trail [trel]: v. 拓墾、闖天下
12. endemic [ɛn`dɛmɪk]: n. 水土不服
13. integral [`ɪntəgrəl]: a. 不可或缺的
14. kaleidoscope [kə`laɪdə.skop]: n. 萬花筒
16. victim [`vɪktɪm]: n. 災民
17. assist [ə`sɪst]: v. 協助
18. relocate [ri`loket]: v. 重新安置（將……）

淡江大學

Tamsui
14

TAMKANG UNIVERSITY

Tamkang University is a non-religious school without strong enterprise subsidies and backup. However, its open academic atmosphere and its "education without walls" philosophy distinguish itself out. In the beginning of founding, the contribution of Tamsui residents couldn't go unnoticed. It began as the Tamkang Junior College of English, founded in 1950 by the father-son duo of Zhang Ming (or Zhang Jiang-Sheng) and Zhang Jian-Bang. In 1958 it was restructured as the Tamkang College of Art and Science, and finally in 1980 it was recertified as Tamkang University. Today Tamkang has campuses in Tamsui, Taipei, and Lanyang, and it has an established online program. It has eight colleges, roughly 27, 000 students, 2, 100 staff and faculty members, and 240, 000 alumni, making it one of the most highly functional and well organized higher education institutions in the world. It has held the title of "The Most Favored Private University by Enterprises" for straight 18 years in The University Guide by Cheers, a magazine that surveyed 2, 000 companies.

The Chinese Palace-style Classrooms

Tamkang University's beautiful scenery and campus has a reputation that extends all over the world, and is a popular place to film movies and TV. One prime example is the Chinese Palace-style classrooms which were built in 1954. They form two parallel structures that reproduce the style of traditional Tang Dynasty typology, with jade green tiles and crimson walls. Along the center is nine ornamental columns and 18 sculpted dragons, each illuminated by two palace-style lanterns. When lighted, the lanterns radiate brilliance that matches the sunset. All of it is the work of Ma Ti-Qian, the first dean of the Department of Architecture. These classrooms have stood for almost 60 years as a wonderful reminder of the past.

Tamkang University Maritime Museum

The Tamkang University Maritime Museum is a detached, 2, 134 square meter building shaped like a ship. It was formerly known as Merchant Ship Hall, one of the top places to learn about navigation and turbines. Zhang Rong-Fa, President of the Evergreen Group, generously donated the facilities. In 1989 government policy was modified so that student recruitment in some fields was suspended. As a result the last group of students graduated in 1989 and Merchant Ship Hall was turned into the Maritime Museum, the first of its kind in Taiwan. The museum showcases ship models from all over the world, both historic and modern, and includes over 50 pieces from Lin Tian-Fu's (the president of the board at the time) personal collection. The museum opened to the public in June of 1990 with no entry fee.

Booklet Square
(or Egg Roll Square)

The predecessor of Booklet Square was a two-story classroom with a courtyard. The classroom was taken down in 1986 and replaced with a square of greens. At the geographical center four pieces of curly building blocks were erected. Designed by Lin Gui-Rong, an architect and alumnus, the arrangement is similar to that of an ancient booklet. So it was named Booklet Square and nicknamed Egg Roll Square due to its curvy appearance, which closely resembled egg rolls. A top down view of the booklet arrangement resembles a motor, which symbolizes the need to continue going forward. The snowy white blocks have a pleasing charm whether under a sapphire blue sky, at sundown, or at night. It is a popular location for school clubs and large-scale activities to take place, and where unforgettable pictures are taken.

Tamkang University's School Anthem

Lyricist / Zou Lu
Melodist / Lui Quan-Sheng

The Tamsui River welcomes ships who have traveled thousands of miles on the ocean blue. Here scholars and noblemen integrate ideas old and new.

Through prudent practice of the proper system, the world can be shaped with knowledge and wisdom.

In the face of success do not succumb to arrogance. Humility and an open mind are the keys to excellence.

You are the best of your generation and the top representatives of a nation.

Lead the way and seize the day!

Dialogue

Q **For 17 years Tamkang University has held the ranking of top private university in Taiwan, and 8th overall in the nation. What an extraordinary job.**

A One of the dominant factors is that Tamkang was the first university of its kind and has earned quite a reputation. Besides the free academic atmosphere, the management is visionary and agile, having had the foresight to focus on globalization, computerization, and futurization many years ago.

Q **Its 240, 000 alumni are a great social resource.**

A It can be translated into a ratio: one to one hundred. This implies that for every 100 Taiwanese, there is one Tamkang graduate, not including their families. They are definitely ideal spokespersons for Tamkang. It's amazing that there are families with three generations of Tamkang graduates.

Q **Tamkang University, founded 60 years ago, usually comes to mind when one talks about Tamsui.**

A Yeah, it surely does. Tamsui is considered by many to be a university town because in addition to Tamkang, it is also home to Aletheia University, St. John's University, the Taipei College of Marine Technology, and Guandu Christ's College.

Q **What do alumni miss most about Tamkang?**

A It must be seeing how the campus changes across the seasons. There is also a Chinese Palace-style classroom with antique lanterns that makes you feel like you've gone back in time. Alumni can relive their student days every March during homecoming.

Q **Tamkang, which is located in the home of folk music, has a thriving musical scene doesn't it?**

A There is a nice auditorium even though Tamkang doesn't have a music department. There is always music on campus and quite a few alumni have become renowned in show business as singers, artists, actors or actresses, and other capacities. There is something about the natural beauty at Tamkang that nurtures artistic students.

Keywords

01. contribution [ˌkɑntrəˈbjuʃən]: n. 貢獻
02. duo [ˈduo]: n. 二人組
04. alumni [əˈlʌmnaɪ]: n. 校友（複數）（alumnus: 男校友 alumna: 女校友）
05. higher education: n. 高等教育
06. survey [səˈve]: v. 調查
07. overall [ˈovəˌɔl]: a. 全面的
08. dominant [ˈdɑmənənt]: a. 佔優勢的、佔首位的
09. academic [ˌækəˈdɛmɪk]: a. 學術的
10. visionary [ˈvɪʒəˌnɛrɪ]: a. 有遠見的
11. agile [ˈædʒaɪl]: a. 輕快的、敏捷的
12. globalize [ˈglobəˌlaɪz]: v. 全球化
13. foresight [ˈforˌsaɪt]: n. 遠見、先見之明

14. spokesperson [`spoks͵pɝsn]: n. 發言人

15. predecessor [`prɛdɪ͵sɛsɚ]: n. 前任、前輩

16. extend [ɪk`stɛnd]: v. 擴大、擴展

17. illuminate [ɪ`lumə͵net]: v. 照亮、照射

18. radiate [`redɪ͵et]: v. 發射（光、熱等）

19. ornamental [͵ɔrnə`mɛntl]: a. 作裝飾用的

20. columns [`kɑləm]: n. 圓柱

21. turbine [`tɝbɪn]: n. 渦輪

河岸自行車道

Tamsui
15

THE BIKEWAY BY THE RIVERBANK

The 2.5-kilometer bikeway by the riverbank that extends from Tamsui to Hongshulin winds its way into Fisherman's Wharf in Tamhai, through the Guandu Bridge, and then into Pali and the Shisanhang Archeology Museum. It's reserved exclusively for pedestrians and cyclists, and the ride is both safe and secure. Exquisite scenery can be enjoyed along the boundless stretches of coastline and thick mangrove while MRT trains speed along overhead. A viewing platform constructed along the bikeway is a great way to see flying egrets, fiddler crabs, mudskippers, and a panorama of the verdant Guan Yin Mountain framed by a brilliant sunset.

Weekend Cycling

The Taipei City government started the bikeway project in 2002. The path was designed to follow along the riverbanks of the Tamsui River, the Keelung River, Jingmei Creek, and Xindian Creek. The 111 kilometer bikeway network covers Jingmei to the south, Neihu to the east, and downstream to the Guandu wetland. Parts of it are named with scenery or location-specific features, such as Guandu Bikeway, the Golden Beach Bikeway, and Pali Bikeway. The scenery and access to nature make biking along the path an ideal leisure activity. Since completion of the bikeway project, weekend cycling has become a national phenomenon.

Biking By the Riverbank

Taiwan is known as the kingdom of bikes whose brand names such as Giant Bicycles and Merida Bikes have ranked among the top ten in the world. Their yearly production numbers over 4.4 million. Many internationally renowned brands have even commissioned bike production in Taiwan. 2.7 million Taiwanese use bikes for exercise and 700, 000 rely on them as a means of transportation. Circling the island by cycling has become a popular pastime. At present 40 bikeways have been laid, totaling about 1, 180 kilometers, most of which are along the water. Take the 60-kilometer Tamsui-Xindian bikeway for example. On the weekends it is full of trendy people who prefer to exercise while maintaining a close connection to the land.

YouBike

Giant Bicycles was commissioned by the Taipei City Government for the construction and operation of YouBike. Their emblem is "U-bike" and their slogan is "YouBike, the Smiley Bike." Trial runs of their unmanned self-service stations took place in March 2009 and service officially began in November 2012. Since then there have been over 130, 000 membership cards issued, over one million rentals, and 158 rental stations established. YouBike operated at a loss until the system became widely established. It is now a unique and ubiquitous part of Taipei city, and their bikes can also be found on the bikeways of Tamsui.

Dialogue

Q **How many days did it take you to cycle around the island?**

A It was a tour of about 900 kilometers that took nine days. But it could be as short as seven, or even five for a professional cyclist. Some daredevil challengers have even set a goal of only three days.

Q **Why is the youth of Taiwan partial to cycling around the island?**

A It is a convenient way to create close ties with our land. It is also widely promoted on the internet that the adoration of Taiwan can be displayed in three physical activities: cycling around the island, hiking the Jade Mountains, and swimming across Sun Moon Lake.

Q Aren't cycling tours carried out by employers to re-mind their employees the importance of maintaining good health?

A One renowned example is that of Liu Jin-Biao, the owner of Giant Bicycles who is in his 70s, who took the lead on several cycling tours around the island with his high ranking employees.

Q YouBike of Taipei City has become quite a sensation, and even got a feature story on Global Traveler.

A Vélib' is a first-of-its-kind public bike sharing program that was started in Paris in 2007 and created a phenomenon across many major cities around the world. YouBike's rental system follows their model and is combined with Easy Card's swipe system.

Q Is YouBike available to foreign tourists?

A Sure, a Metro Easy Card and registration at the service column are all that's required.

Keywords

01. pedestrian [pə`dɛstrɪən]: n. 行人
02. cyclist [`saɪk!ɪst]: n. 自行車騎士
03. mudskipper [mʌd `skɪp ə]: n. 彈塗魚
04. daredevil [`dɛr͵dɛv!]: a. 蠻勇的、不怕死的
05. to maintain good health: v. 養生
06. sensation [sɛn`seʃən]: n. 轟動的事件
07. phenomenon [fə`namə͵nan]: n. 稀有的現象
08. swipe [swaɪp] system: n. 刷卡系統
09. ubiquitous [ju`bɪkwətəs]: a. 普遍存在的
10. unmanned [͵ʌn`mænd]: a. 無人的、無人駕駛的
11. trial [`traɪəl] run: n. 試營運
12. commissioned [kə`mɪʃənd]: a. 受委任的

參考資料

淡江大學文學院，《金色記憶：淡水學用與辭典》，淡大，2002。

莊展鵬主編，《台灣深度旅遊手冊 2: 淡水》，遠流，1990。

廖文卿主編，《淡水不思議》，新北市立淡水古蹟博物館，2013。

趙莒玲，《淡水心靈地圖》，黎明，2005

新北市政府官網：www.ntpc.gov.tw

淡水區公所官網：http: //www.tamsui.ntpc.gov.tw

話說淡水

話說淡水

話說淡水

話說淡水

話說淡水

話說淡水

國家圖書館出版品預行編目資料

話說淡水 / 吳錫德編著；吳岳峰翻譯. -- 初版. -- 新北
市：淡大出版中心, 2015.04
　　面；　公分. --（淡江書系；TB005）
中英對照
ISBN 978-986-5982-75-1(平裝)
1.人文地理 2.新北市淡水區
733.9/103.9/141.4　　　　　　　　103027049

淡江書系 TB005

話說淡水
Let's talk about Tamsui　【中文英文對照】

作　　　者	吳錫德
譯　　　者	吳岳峰
插　　　圖	陳吉斯
攝　　　影	吳秋霞、林盈均、邱逸清、周伯謙、陳美聖、馮文星
封面設計	斐類設計工作室
美術編輯	葉武宗
中文錄音	張書瑜、張柏緯
英文錄音	吳岳峰、李怡潔
影音剪輯	方舟軟體有限公司 - 陳雅文
印刷廠	中茂分色製版有限公司

發 行 人	張家宜
社　　　長	林信成
總 編 輯	吳秋霞
執行編輯	張瑜倫
出 版 者	淡江大學出版中心
出版日期	**2015年4月**
版　　　次	初版
定　　　價	**360元**

總 經 銷	紅螞蟻圖書有限公司
展 售 處	**淡江大學出版中心**
	地址：新北市25137 淡水區英專路151號海博館1樓
	電話：02-86318661　　傳真：02-86318660
	淡江大學—驚聲書城
	新北市淡水區英專路151號商管大樓3樓
	電話：02-26217840